AF410298

THE NUMBER NOBODY TALKS ABOUT

HOW TO PREPARE, PRICE, AND SELL YOUR BOUTIQUE FITNESS STUDIO

MITCH MCGINLEY

*For Karson—my partner in every sense of the word.
Thank you for making all of my dreams come true.*

*And for every studio owner who has poured
their life into their community, and
wonders what comes next.*

This book is for you.

A NOTE BEFORE WE BEGIN

I am not an attorney, a CPA, or a licensed financial advisor. Nothing in this book constitutes tax, legal, or investment advice for your specific situation. Where this book discusses legal concepts—employment classification, lease assignment, representations and warranties, indemnification, non-compete agreements, and related topics—it reflects general market practice and my experience. It does not reflect the law of any specific state; individual deals vary significantly, and the law itself changes. Always work with a qualified M&A attorney before signing anything.

The information here reflects my professional experience as a consultant, business broker, and exit planning advisor who has engaged with thousands of boutique fitness studio owners all over the world. We have closed more than seventy successful transactions, almost entirely within the boutique fitness industry. Yet every business and every transaction is still different.

For matters specific to your business, including tax strategy, legal agreements, employment compliance, and financial planning, please work with qualified professionals in those fields. It's always a team effort, and every player has a key role.

The case studies and client stories shared here are real. Identifying details have been changed to protect client confidentiality.

TABLE OF CONTENTS

INTRODUCTION: MY FAVORITE DEAL

This is my best story. It was December 20th, 2024, ten days before my family moved to Spain. The founder of a big marketing firm called me about a client who needed help. The seller, "Michelle," was a multi-unit Club Pilates owner who had been negotiating privately with a single buyer for over a year.

Twelve months of meetings, document requests, updates, delays—and ultimately a final offer far below where the conversation started. She was exhausted, depressed, and days away from accepting it.

We both knew she deserved $1,000,000 more. I was certain I could make it happen if she'd give me time. She was scared, though. She didn't want to lose the buyer she had in hand. She'd been through hell for a year trying to make that deal work. So she gave me four days to bring her a better offer. Four days!

I did it. Michelle walked away two months later with $600,000 more (after fees and taxes).

I'll come back to this story in Chapter Fifteen, but I'm telling it now because it captures everything this book is about: what's possible when you approach the sale of your business with the right preparation, strategy, and support.

THE CHALLENGE

Only one in five businesses listed for sale actually sells, a figure drawn from BizBuySell's transaction data and cited in *Forbes* (February 2017). Four out of five walk away with nothing. And their biggest asset—the community they spent years building—simply disappears.

WHAT BROUGHT ME HERE

I want to change that—at least within boutique fitness, the niche I know and love. My name is Mitch McGinley. Like most people in our industry, I started somewhere in corporate America, found yoga after an injury, and then just stayed. I originally started in hotel management, moved into operations and finance, and ended up running a startup that bought and sold boutique hotels across San Diego. That's where I learned business transactions from the inside. What makes a business attractive to buy. How to spot unrealized value. What actually happens from listing to closing.

But I was working too many hours for someone else's benefit. My wife Karson and I were newly married, wanting to start a family and create a different kind of life. So when the owner of our neighborhood yoga studio asked us if we'd buy it, we said yes without hesitation. I walked out of the hotel and straight into entrepreneurship. The day after, we found out we were pregnant with our first child.

The early years were as hard as you'd expect. I knew operations and finance, but I didn't know what it felt like to manage compliance, taxes, leases, landlords, and the endless parade of software and marketing vendors. I learned it all the hard way, the way you probably did, too. What I brought was operational discipline and top-shelf customer service. What Karson brought was everything else—the talent, the draw, and the ability to inspire and lead. She doesn't get enough credit here, but it's important to acknowledge that none of this would have been possible without her.

Within a couple of years, I started consulting alongside the studio. My friend and colleague Laura Munkholm connected me with Mindbody's education team, and I became a founding faculty member for Mindbody University. I connected with the best owners and consultants in the industry by speaking at conferences and traveling the world. Those experiences accelerated my understanding of the industry as a whole. I started seeing the patterns that separated thriving businesses from struggling ones. And I was able to help countless studio owners become better business people.

Everything seemed to be going great when someone approached us about selling. It ended up being something of a disaster. The conversation lasted six months, and it didn't work out at all. But going through that process showed us everything that we needed to do to be more successful.

So we went back to running the studio. We fixed everything. Cleaned up the books, strengthened the team, renegotiated the lease, and made sure two more years of tax returns reflected real profitability. The second time, we sold for five times what we'd paid—a multiple that reflected our hard work and preparation.

After that, all of my friends and colleagues in the industry started asking for help with selling their businesses. I found a unique niche. No one had combined deep industry knowledge with real transaction expertise. Industry consultants didn't understand transactions. Generalist brokers aren't familiar with the nuances of boutique fitness.

In 2020, I created Boutique Fitness Broker. In 2023, my friend and colleague Kristin Abel joined me as a partner. Kristin deserves tremendous credit here—she is a former CPA and yoga studio owner whom I helped exit in 2022. From here on, when I say "we," I mean Kristin and me. After four years of doing this work side by side, it is genuinely ours.

We've helped more than seventy owners sell their businesses, with a close rate of around 80 percent—four times the industry average. We've transacted nearly $30 million. When done right, these businesses typically sell for $300,000 to $500,000 per location. Some lower, some higher, but everything in this book applies to all.

People ask me all the time what I do for a living. When I say I help studio owners sell their businesses, the response is sometimes a raised eyebrow, followed by something like, "That's specific; I never knew you could sell those."

Yes, you absolutely can. And for significant sums of money. But you have to prepare and have a plan for it.

I've spent the last ten years traveling to conferences and speaking with studio owners all over the world, and I keep encountering the same patterns. Brilliant, passionate operators who have built real, profitable businesses but have no idea how to exit. Owners who have been told by someone that their business is "worth" some number with no basis in market reality. Owners who have neglected a lease for years and are suddenly facing a landlord who has all the power. Owners who have underreported income on their taxes and now can't prove to a lender what the business actually earned.

When done right, selling your business is a win-win-win. The seller gets paid and enjoys a well-deserved break before whatever comes next. The buyer gets to invest in themselves and grow something real. And the community continues to thrive.

Everything I know about preparing, positioning, and selling a boutique fitness business is in these pages. It doesn't matter whether you plan to sell in two years or in ten. You built something worth preserving. It's likely your largest asset. Let's make sure you get everything you deserve. For yourself, for your team, and for your community.

PART I

PREPARATION DETERMINES PRICE

1

YOU DESERVE TO GET PAID

Most sellers I meet don't fully appreciate what they've built. They think of their work as a service, not a business—something that comes from the heart and doesn't deserve a big payday. I love that about this industry. The owners are among the most passionate and kind people I've ever met. They're in it because they want to help people feel happier, healthier, and stronger. They aren't usually driven by money.

But you didn't just help people. You didn't just teach classes and collect membership fees. You built a "third place"—the community anchor between home and work, a mental health resource, a space where people show up on their worst days and leave feeling human again. A place where people walk in stressed, late for class, wearing everything they're going through—and walk out with tears on their cheeks and the kind of smile that comes from somewhere deep. You made that possible.

It just so happens you also built a sustainable, reliable business that has real, transferable financial value—and you deserve to get paid for it. Because we all know you probably haven't gotten paid enough along the way.

I've talked to thousands of buyers. I know what keeps them up at night. If you understand their fears, you'll understand exactly what you need to fix.

"What happens when the owner leaves?" This is the single most common concern. Buyers have seen it—the charismatic founder who IS the brand, who teaches the most popular classes, who every member adores, who could leave and take half the membership with them. Buyers don't want to buy a person. They want to buy a system.

"Are these numbers real?" Buyers know that small business owners minimize profit on their tax returns. They come in skeptical, and any inconsistency amplifies that skepticism into alarm. One accounting error, one misclassified expense, one year where your numbers don't line up—and the whole deal can unravel.

"What's going to happen with the landlord?" A studio without a usable lease is a studio with no location. No location, no business.

"Will the staff stay?" Your team is the living infrastructure of your business. A talented GM, a beloved lead instructor, a reliable front-desk person who knows every member by name—none of that is replaceable overnight.

THE PART NOBODY WANTS TO HEAR

You will almost certainly walk away with less money than you wanted. Not because you were taken advantage of, but because the gap between what we imagine our life's work is worth and what the market will actually pay is almost always larger than we expect.

Then there are taxes.

Here's what I know: once the shock of that transition fades—and it always fades—sellers always say it was worth it. The money was real. The freedom was real. The relief was real. The joy that the legacy and community live on is real.

The goal of this book isn't to set you up for a fairy tale. It's to help you get the best outcome available to you—which, when done right, is life-changing money and freedom for whatever comes next.

If you want a snapshot of where you stand right now, start with the checklist in Appendix A. It'll tell you more about your exit readiness than anything else you can do in the next hour.

WHY SELLING FEELS LIKE A BETRAYAL

The weight of everything you've already put in makes it hard to imagine letting go. There's always that voice: "You're not supposed to sell this business—you're supposed to fix what's broken, grow it, get to the next level, and then you can think about it."

There's also a cultural taboo in fitness around talking about selling. These businesses are built on mission and community. Talking about monetizing your exit can feel like you're reducing your community to a line item on a balance sheet.

Let me push back on that. Selling your business responsibly—finding the right buyer, getting fair value, ensuring continuity for your staff and members—is not a betrayal of your mission. It's an expression of it. You built something worth preserving. Selling it right means the thing you built continues after you.

THE CONVERSATION AT HOME

Before the conversation with your staff, before the conversation with your GM, before any of the professional conversations this book prepares you for, there is usually a harder one. The one at the kitchen table with the person or people who have been living in this business alongside you, even when they weren't there every day.

For most of the sellers I work with, their families have built their lives around this business. The schedule, the income, the social calendar, the identity it gave them. When you say you're thinking about selling, you're not just talking about a business transaction. You're telling them a chapter of your shared life is coming to an end. The Saturday morning rhythm and the member holiday parties and the way people talk about your family at school pickup—all of it will be different.

Some family members will be relieved. They've watched you carry this for years, and they're ready to watch you put it down. Some will be anxious about the financial change. Some will grieve the community and the identity the business gave them, too—because it did, whether or not they worked in it. Most will feel some combination of all of these things simultaneously.

Important questions to ask: What would life look like on the other side of this? What are we hoping for? When is the right time? What is the right number? Who is the right person? What comes next? What are we afraid of? Those conversations, had early and honestly, mean that by the time the process starts, the energy is moving in the right direction. And when the loneliness of the active sale process arrives— and it will—there is someone at home who actually understands what you're carrying.

This isn't a business transaction conversation. It's a life transition conversation. Have it first.

WHEN PARTNERS DISAGREE

What I've described above is the best case—multiple people moving in the same direction. But sometimes they aren't.

I've worked with sellers whose partners weren't ready. One business partner or spouse sees the finish line, and the other sees a cliff. One is excited about freedom; the other is terrified of what will happen to the income, the identity, the schedule that holds their family together. These conversations can get painful fast, and they often surface things that have nothing to do with the business—unspoken anxieties about money, about control, about what happens to the relationship when the thing that structured your shared life disappears.

My guidance: don't force it. If your partner isn't there yet, slow down. Bring them into the whole picture—show them the real numbers, the net proceeds, what life looks like on the other side. Sometimes resistance melts when abstract fear meets concrete math. Sometimes it doesn't, and you need more time. A sale that fractures your life is not a successful exit, regardless of the price.

The sellers who handle this well are the ones who explore all the feelings first. Treat the disagreement as data, not betrayal. Your partner's fear is telling you something—about what they need to feel safe. Listen to it.

2

EXIT PLANNING STARTS NOW

Exit planning is the most overlooked idea in boutique fitness. Most studio owners got into this industry driven by passion—for movement, for community, for helping people feel better. That passion is what makes this industry special. But passion is not a business strategy, and it won't get you paid when it's time to move on.

The owners I've worked with who got the best outcomes—three to four times earnings, multiple buyers competing, real financial freedom—almost all had one thing in common: they planned for their exit.

WHAT EXIT PLANNING ACTUALLY MEANS

Exit planning doesn't mean obsessing over your exit in year one. It means making decisions with one eye on transferability. It's the kind of thing that should always be simmering in the back of your mind, influencing decisions day to day.

Every time you're tempted to run a personal expense through the business but don't—that's exit planning. Every time you're deciding between the cheapest instructor and the best one—that's exit planning. Every time your lease comes up for renewal, and you're tempted to take a short-term extension because it's easier—exit planning.

A business built with the exit in mind is almost always a better business. The discipline it requires—clean financials, documented systems, a strong team, a solid lease—makes the business more valuable, whether you sell it or not.

THE UPSIDE OF THINKING AHEAD

Every time I raise the topic of thinking ahead with a studio owner, the response is some version of: "Sure, I know I should be thinking about this, but..."

The "but" is always the same. Too much going on. The business needs attention. There's a staff issue, a lease problem, a membership slump. Exit planning feels like planning for a future that's far away, and the present always wins.

Here's what I tell them: the owners who are always too busy to think about exit planning are the ones trapped in their businesses the longest. They can't leave because the business needs them. They can't sell because the business isn't sellable without them. They work longer than they wanted to, earn less than they should, and end up exhausted and bitter when they finally get out.

The owners who think about it—even just one or two decisions a year with transferability in mind—create options.

TWO YEARS BUYS YOU OPTIONS

The sooner you start, the better. I always emphasize a two-year head start. That's enough time for two more clean tax returns to tell the real story of your earnings. Enough time to hire and develop the right people while extricating yourself from the business. Enough time to renegotiate your lease before it's too late. More runway means more options, and more options mean better outcomes.

Here's what sellers who plan ahead understand: time is not just a resource—it's a multiplier. Every year of genuine preparation—cleaner books, stronger team, better lease—increases both your SDE and your multiple simultaneously. A $50,000 improvement in annual earnings while elevating your leadership team could add another $150,000 to $200,000 to your sale price.

FROM $1.5 MILLION TO $3 MILLION IN EIGHTEEN MONTHS

When I talk about planning two years out, "Jennifer" is the proof. Jennifer is a contemporary Pilates studio owner who came to me right after opening her second location.

She had opened her first studio during the worst of COVID, when everyone thought she was crazy. She signed a lease on a space another business had abandoned, negotiated extraordinary terms from a desperate landlord, and opened with a waiting list she'd built entirely through Instagram. By the time she called me, she had a thriving first location and had just opened number two. She wasn't burned out. She wasn't in crisis. She just knew she was getting tired and wanted to get out while everything was strong.

We worked together for a few weeks. I walked her through the five elements—team, systems, customer base, lease, and financials. Her lease was a strength: long-term, favorable economics and a clean assignment clause. Her financials were a weakness: a bookkeeper who wasn't doing proper accounting, and two years of tax returns that understated her real profitability because she'd been aggressive about deductions. Her team and systems had room to expand—too much of the day-to-day still relied on her. But the customers were loyal and growing.

I told her to give it two years. Fix the books. Prove the second location was as profitable as the first. Hire a GM. Extract yourself from the day-to-day. Wean off the personal training clients and develop other teachers to lead the teacher training. Two more clean tax returns, and the value of the business would double.

She did it in eighteen months. Crushed it. When we went to market, the valuation had doubled—from $1.5 million to $3 million.

Jennifer had seven offers. We leveraged them against each other, and she sold to her favorite buyer—no SBA required—at the price she wanted, all cash at closing. She walked away with enough to buy a house outright and fund whatever dream comes next. Her studio continues to thrive. Her staff is still happily employed. The business is growing. Everyone wins.

THE VALUE YOU HAVEN'T REALIZED YET

I grew up in a bubble where people only talked about two kinds of investments: real estate and stocks. Nobody talked about buying, building, and selling businesses as a strategy, even though—for most of the people I've worked with—their businesses are their largest assets.

If you own a profitable business, you are sitting on an asset that a buyer would normally pay two to four times your annual earnings to own. The math is covered in Chapter Four. For now, the point is simpler: the business you built has a number attached to it, and that number is almost certainly larger than you think.

3

WHAT BUYERS ARE ACTUALLY BUYING

What you are selling—what a buyer is actually acquiring—comes down to five elements: your team, your systems, your customer base, your lease, and your financial records.

When all five are strong, your business commands a premium price. When any of them are weak, you either fix them before you sell or accept a discount—if you can sell at all.

Part One of this book covers each of these five elements in depth. Everything in this book points back to them. And the business model itself is on your side. Your members have given you their credit card and said they're in. They're enrolled, committed, and habitual. Even through recessions and crises, people keep their fitness memberships when they cut everything else. That resilience has real asset value.

A few years ago, I worked with a yoga studio owner outside Austin who had built one of the best-run small businesses I'd ever seen. Strong membership, loyal staff, clean books, and a lease with seven years remaining. She had done everything right. When we went to market, I expected multiple offers and a clean process.

Instead, buyers expressed interest, scheduled visits, reviewed the financials—and then went quiet. One by one. The business was performing well. The price was fair. So what was going wrong?

When I debriefed the buyers who passed, the answer was consistent: the owner taught twelve classes a week. She was the most popular instructor by far. Her name was on the website as the face of the brand. Members mentioned her unprompted when describing why they loved the studio. Buyers were terrified that without her, the membership would walk.

We pulled the business off the market, restructured her class schedule over six months—four classes, then two, then a mentoring role—and relaunched with eighteen months of membership data showing the transition hadn't hurt retention. When we went back to market, the same business sold for roughly 20 percent above our original target, in less than sixty days. We addressed the one thing buyers feared. They responded accordingly.

This illustrates a fundamental point: buyers are not just evaluating your financial statements. They're evaluating the risk that what makes your business special doesn't survive your departure. Each of the five elements matters in practice.

THE TEAM

The single most valuable hire you can make before going to market is a general manager—someone who runs the day-to-day without you. We'll explore this topic in depth in Chapter Seven. For now, you should understand that if a buyer asks, "Who would run this place if you weren't here?" and the answer is, "I'd have to hire someone," you've told them they're buying a job, not a business.

Beyond the GM, buyers are looking at the depth of the instructor team. Is your lead instructor's schedule fully booked? Great—but what happens if they leave? Is there someone who can step into their classes and retain the members? The loss of any one person can't collapse the business.

Staff longevity matters too. A team that's been together for three or more years signals stability, culture, and low turnover risk. A team that cycles every year signals a management problem that the buyer will have to solve.

THE SYSTEMS

Buyers are acquiring your systems as much as they are acquiring your revenue. Systems are what make a business transferable—the documented processes, software, and playbooks that let someone new step in and run things.

Your studio management software is the first place a buyer looks. Your CRM needs to be clean, current, and fully populated with accurate member data. A buyer's due diligence team will spend time in this system. Membership count, retention rate, revenue per member, attendance trends—all of it comes from your software, and it needs to match what you've told them.

Then there's the operational documentation. Do you have a staff onboarding manual? A customer service playbook? A procedure for handling membership disputes, injury incidents, or instructor no-shows? These don't need to be elaborate—but they need to exist. A buyer who can hand something to a new GM and say, "Here's how this place runs" is buying something real. A buyer who has to figure it out from scratch is buying a project, and they'll price it accordingly.

THE CLIENTS

Three numbers define the health of your customer base in a buyer's eyes: new visits, conversion, and retention.

Active membership is straightforward—how many people are paying you right now. But buyers push past that number quickly. What's the trend? Is membership growing, stable, or declining? A declining roster, even one that's still profitable, signals a headwind the buyer will have to reverse.

Retention rate tells buyers how committed your community actually is. If you're losing 50 percent of your members every year and replacing them through marketing, that's a different business than a studio where members average two or three years. High retention means lower acquisition costs, a stronger community, and a business that's less dependent on the owner's personal magnetism. Long-tenured members are also less likely to churn when ownership changes. They're there for the community and the habit, not just for you.

THE LEASE

Buyers want at least three years remaining, but five or ten is much better. They need the lease to be assignable—transferable to a new owner with the landlord's approval. They want rent within market range, not so high that the economics are compromised, and not so low that the landlord has an incentive to decline assignment and re-lease at market rate.

Chapter Six is dedicated entirely to lease dynamics because it's that important. What I'll say here is that if you haven't looked at your lease recently, do so this week. Understand your "Assignment and Subletting" clause, your renewal options, and your rent escalation schedule. Any serious buyer will scrutinize these, and surprises in the lease are among the most common deal killers I encounter.

THE FINANCIAL RECORDS

Clean, verifiable financial records are the foundation of any sale. The valuation, the financing, the buyer's confidence—all of it depends on those records.

We'll cover the financial details in Chapter Five. For now, here's what matters most: the number buyers and lenders care about is not your net income. It's your Seller's Discretionary Earnings—the real cash the business generates for its owner, after adjusting for owner compensation, non-recurring expenses, and personal items run through the business. The integrity of that calculation is what makes or breaks your deal. (See Appendix B for a glossary of key terms, including SDE.)

WHAT'S ACTUALLY INCLUDED IN THE SALE

There's a question most first-time sellers haven't thought through: what exactly are you selling? The answer is more nuanced than it seems, and getting clear on it early prevents surprises later.

In a standard asset sale—the structure used in most boutique fitness transactions—you're selling specific assets, not the legal entity itself. You and your attorney will produce a schedule that defines exactly what transfers. Here's what that typically includes, and what to watch out for in each category:

PHYSICAL ASSETS:

- All-owned equipment (Reformers, Bikes, Weights, Sound Systems, Mirrors, Furniture, Front Desk Hardware)

These transfer cleanly if they're owned outright. Equipment under a lease or financing agreement is different. Either the balance gets paid off through closing, or that lease has to be assigned to the buyer, and the equipment lender has to consent, just like a real estate landlord. Many owners are surprised to discover that their reformers are financed and that the lender has transfer restrictions. Know before you list.

DIGITAL ASSETS:

- Your website and domain name
- Your email list and CRM database
- Your Google Business profile and reviews
- Your branded email address
- Social media accounts.

All of these have real value and all transfer, but they require deliberate handling in the purchase agreement. Software and subscriptions are often annoying. The profile may be registered under your personal Google account, and transferring it requires specific steps. Don't assume your buyer will figure it out after closing. The handover is handled together usually the day of or after closing (sharing credentials and updating contact information). If your personal identity is deeply intertwined with a studio account (if you are the account), that's worth addressing before going to market.

INTELLECTUAL PROPERTY:

- Your studio name and associated trademarks
- Your proprietary class names or formats
- Your branded materials
- Your teacher training curriculum

If a training program is tied to your personal credentials, the buyer needs to understand what happens to it after you leave. That affects its value as a transferable asset.

WHAT'S NOT INCLUDED:

- Cash in your bank accounts
- Receivables already collected before closing (if any)
- Any liabilities the buyer isn't explicitly assuming

The Purchase Agreement will define all of this, but walking in with a clear inventory of what you own—physical, digital, and intellectual— puts you in a better position to negotiate what transfers and at what value. Most sellers have never made that list. Make it this week.

4

WORTH IS THE WRONG WORD

I try to avoid the word "worth." It means something different to every buyer and seller, and so it's not mine to define.

Every seller I work with arrives at our first conversation with a number in mind. It's usually round, optimistic, and comes with a shrug. It's almost never rooted in market realities.

"Potential" is not a valuation methodology.

The market has its own methodology—and it's the only one that matters when you're trying to sell. It's systematic and learnable, and once you understand it, you'll look at your business differently—as the financial asset it actually is, rather than the emotional labor it sometimes feels like.

TWO NUMBERS, ONE EQUATION

Boutique fitness businesses are valued as a multiple of Seller's Discretionary Earnings, or SDE. The formula is simple:

Valuation = SDE x Multiple

Everything else in this chapter is about understanding those two terms—and what you can actually do to increase them.

WHAT SDE ACTUALLY MEANS

SDE is your business's true operating profit—the real cash it generates for its owner, after adjusting for things that won't exist under new ownership.

You start with your reported net income. Then you add back owner compensation (the adjustment can be positive or negative, depending on how much you pay yourself). Add back depreciation and amortization (non-cash accounting items), personal expenses you've been running through the business—your car, your health insurance, meals, and travel that were personal—and any one-time expenses that won't recur.

The resulting number is SDE. It represents the economic benefit the business delivers to its owner. If your SDE is $250,000, a buyer is acquiring the right to receive $250,000 a year from running this business.

A REAL SDE CALCULATION

- **Gross Revenue..................$620,000**
- Cost of Goods Sold (Retail).......$18,000
- *Gross Profit.................................$602,000*
- Rent...$72,000
- Payroll....................................$198,000
- Owner Salary..........................$48,000
- Marketing...............................$24,000
- Software & Subscriptions.........$9,600
- Insurance.................................$7,200
- Utilities...................................$8,800
- Supplies & Maintenance..........$6,000
- Professional Fees.....................$8,800
- Meals & Entertainment...........$4,200
- Auto Expense...........................$6,000
- Depreciation...........................$12,000

- Owner's Health Insurance.......$14,800
- *Total Expenses.............................$419,400*
- **Net Income...........................$182,600**
- *Addbacks and Adjustments*
- Owner's Salary.........................$48,000
- Auto Expense............................$6,000
- Meals & Entertainment.............$4,200
- Depreciation............................$12,000
- Personal legal............................$3,500
- Owner's Health Insurance......$14,800
- *Total Addbacks..............................$88,500*
- **Adjusted Earnings (SDE).......$271,100**

At a 3x multiple, this studio is valued at approximately $813,300. At 2x, it's $542,200. The difference between those two multiples—$271,100—is determined by the strength of your team, your lease, your systems, and your member retention. That's what Part One of this book is about.

THE ART OF THE MULTIPLE

Two businesses with identical SDE can sell at very different prices. The reason is the multiple. It reflects the market's assessment of the reliability, sustainability, and desirability of that income stream.

For smaller, single-location studios, multiples typically range from 2x to 3x SDE. Larger, multi-location operations with strong systems, diverse revenue streams, and institutional buyer interest can command higher prices. I've seen 5x in only two of my deals and both businesses were growing rapidly. It's rare. The $1 million to $5 million deals usually land between 3.5x and 4.5x.

Factors that push your multiple higher include consistent revenue growth (even 10 percent year-over-year changes how buyers see you), high member retention, a management team that doesn't need the owner, a lease with many years remaining at favorable economics, and diversified revenue—memberships plus retail plus private sessions plus corporate wellness contracts. Every class you teach is a class a buyer worries about losing. So systematically extract yourself from the operational and instructional core of the business in the two years before you sell.

Factors that push your multiple down include owner-dependent revenue, high staff turnover, a short or problematic lease, declining membership trends, revenue concentration in one or two services, or financial records that are difficult to verify.

But here's what the formula misses: the multiple you actually receive also depends on how many buyers are competing for your business. All the strategic improvements establish your floor. Competition is what drives the price above it. We'll cover this topic in further detail in Chapter Fifteen.

WHAT YOU CONTROL AND WHAT YOU DON'T

This is worth being explicit about, because the SDE-times-multiple formula can make it feel like your outcome is a math problem you can solve. It's not—it's half math and half market.

You control your SDE. Clean books, proper addbacks, two years of verifiable tax returns—that's preparation, and it's entirely in your hands. Part One of this book is about maximizing that number.

You influence your multiple. A strong team, a long lease, high retention, diversified revenue, and low owner dependence all push your multiple higher. But you don't set the multiple—buyers do, based on how much risk they see. Two identical businesses with the same SDE will sell at different multiples depending on how many buyers are competing and how confident those buyers feel. Part Two of this book is about creating that competition.

The combination is where the real outcome lives. You do the work to make the business worth buying. Then you run a process that makes buyers compete to buy it. Neither half works without the other.

THE CEILING AND HOW TO BREAK THROUGH IT

Most buyers finance the deal through the SBA 7(a) loan program, which creates a practical ceiling on how high SBA-financed deals can go—typically around 3x to 3.5x SDE. We'll review those mechanics in detail in Chapter Nineteen.

5

THE NUMBER YOUR ACCOUNTANT NEVER TOLD YOU ABOUT

My client, "Lisa," owned a multi-location franchise that, by most measures, was phenomenal. Strong membership, loyal staff, corner of the market in a major city. When we ran the SDE calculation, the business showed a little over $1,000,000 in adjusted earnings. At an optimistic 5x multiple, that's a business valued around $5,000,000.

One problem. Lisa's bookkeeper had switched accounting methods mid-year—from cash basis to accrual—without properly restating the prior year. The result was a 16 percent gap between what last year showed and what it should have shown. The buyer's forensic accountant caught it. Their revised offer came back more than 20 percent lower—roughly $1,000,000 less than what we'd been working toward.

The conversations that followed dragged on for ninety days before the deal fell apart. Not because Lisa was dishonest. Because her financial records were inconsistent in ways that neither she nor her bookkeeper caught until it was too late.

I tell this story because I want you to feel the stakes before we get into the mechanics. Your financial records are not an administrative chore. They are the primary documentation of your business's value, and their quality determines—more than almost any other factor—what you will receive for your life's work.

THREE DOCUMENTS, ONE STORY

Three documents drive your valuation and your ability to get a deal financed:

Federal tax returns for the past three years. This is the gold standard. A bank underwriting an SBA loan will look at your business tax return and verify that it generates enough real income to service the loan payments. Returns that show low income—because you've been aggressive about deductions, running personal expenses through the business, managing taxes rather than reporting reality—create a financing ceiling that may be lower than what your business actually deserves.

Monthly profit-and-loss statements for the trailing twenty-four months. Prepared by your bookkeeper, these show the month-by-month story of your revenue and expenses. Buyers will look at trends, seasonality, and unusual fluctuations. Make sure these are accurate, consistent with your tax returns, and produced using proper accounting methodology.

Bank statements for the past twenty-four months. These are the raw data that everything else is supposed to match. When a buyer's accountant reconciles your P&L against your bank statements, and they don't agree, that's when questions get asked, timelines get extended, and prices get renegotiated.

THE TRADEOFF THAT COMES BACK TO BITE YOU

This is the single most common financial problem I encounter.

Many studio owners—particularly those with good accountants who specialize in minimizing tax liability—have spent years legally reducing their taxable income. Rational while you're operating. A problem when it's time to sell. The same tax returns that minimized your tax bill will now limit how much a bank will lend a buyer to purchase your business.

The SDE calculation partially addresses this. When we calculate your real earnings, we add back owner salary, personal expenses (meals, travel, auto), depreciation, and interest, and the resulting number may be substantially higher than what your tax returns show. This is legitimate, and good buyers and lenders understand it.

But the addback process has limits. You can't add back something you can't document. If you've been running personal expenses through the business without categorizing them clearly, a buyer's accountant will challenge every addback and may not accept undocumented ones. If the gap between your addback-adjusted SDE and your reported tax income is large, banks get nervous. The more you have to explain, the faster buyers lose trust.

The solution, if you have two or more years before you plan to sell: work with your CPA to shift your tax strategy. Show more profit. Pay more taxes now to receive more at closing. The math almost always works in your favor—an extra $10,000 of reported profit generates $30,000 in additional sale price at a 3x multiple. The tax on that $10,000 is probably $3,000, depending on your bracket. Run the exact numbers with your CPA for your specific entity structure and state. But paying $3,000 in taxes to unlock $30,000 in valuation is an easy trade.

If you're already close to market and the tax history is what it is, work with a quality-of-earnings firm to build the most compelling, fully documented addback schedule possible. There's usually more value to unlock, even when the books aren't pretty—but it takes an independent third party to give buyers trust.

THIS IS FIXABLE

If you don't have one yet, hire a firm specializing in small-business bookkeeping and accounting. The categorization of expenses, the management of owner addbacks, the treatment of equipment depreciation, and the consistency of accounting method across years—all of these affect how your financials look to a buyer and how much they're willing to pay. You need someone who has seen a transaction from the inside.

A clean set of books means no personal expenses buried in ambiguous categories, no large miscellaneous expense lines a buyer can't verify, no accounting method changes without proper documentation, and no material discrepancies between what the P&L shows and what the bank statements and tax returns confirm.

GIFT CARDS AND OUTSTANDING PACKAGES: THE LIABILITY THAT TRANSFERS

Every unredeemed gift card and prepaid class package in your system is a liability that transfers to the buyer. They inherit the obligation to deliver those sessions at no additional revenue to them, and they will put a number on it. I've seen this liability run into six figures for studios that sell large packages at premium rates.

Know your number before you go to market. Pull a report from your studio management software showing the total value of all unredeemed packages and gift cards. Then understand how it gets handled in your deal—usually a downward purchase price adjustment or a credit to the buyer at closing. What you want to avoid is discovering this number for the first time in due diligence, when you've lost the leverage to frame it favorably.

If you have time, reduce the balance: migrate clients from large packages toward monthly memberships, encourage existing package holders to use their sessions, and stop selling large blocks. A smaller outstanding balance is a cleaner deal.

THIRD-PARTY PLATFORM AGREEMENTS: WHAT TRANSFERS AND WHAT DOESN'T

Third-party platform agreements are another hidden transfer risk. ClassPass, Mindbody Marketplace, Gympass, and similar platforms often have agreements that are non-transferable—when your studio sells, the agreement terminates, and the new owner has to reapply under potentially different terms. If a platform represents 10 or 15 percent of your revenue, a buyer who discovers this in due diligence will either reprice the deal or walk.

Audit every platform agreement before going to market. For each one, ask: Is it assignable? What happens at a change of ownership? What percentage of revenue does it represent? Disclose it in your CIM and have a proposed treatment ready. Sophisticated buyers will find this regardless—being the one who surfaces it first is the stronger position.

THE INVESTMENT THAT INSTILLS CONFIDENCE

A quality of earnings review—a QoE—is an independent accounting analysis that verifies your financials and produces an adjusted earnings figure you and your buyer can both stand behind.

Historically, QoEs were commissioned by buyers during due diligence. Increasingly, sophisticated sellers commission them before going to market. A seller-commissioned QoE does two things: it tells you the real SDE of your business (which is often different from what you thought), and it tells every buyer that the financials have already been verified by a third party. This reduces due diligence friction, compresses the timeline, and signals confidence that makes buyers comfortable paying premium prices.

QoEs from reputable firms typically cost $10,000 to $20,000+, depending on complexity. It's worth every dollar. Compare that to waiting for your buyer to pay for one after you've gone exclusive—and the real risk of a surprise in due diligence forcing renegotiation. If you're not sure where to start, ask your bookkeeper one question: Have you ever worked on a business sale? The answer will tell you what you need to know.

6

LEASE & LANDLORD: THE DEAL'S BIGGEST WILDCARD

I could tell stories of my landlord trauma for days. Here are the ones that matter most.

A client once came to me with a business that, by every operational measure, was extraordinary. Her yoga studio had been running for nine years. She had 400 members, a GM who ran the day-to-day flawlessly, and two years of clean financials showing $240,000 in SDE. We went to market at a target price of $720,000. Within three weeks, we had two serious buyers. The process was going exactly as it should.

Then we approached the landlord about the assignment.

He said he'd consent—but at a 60 percent rent increase. The monthly rent would jump from $6,200 to $9,900. At that new rent level, the business's SDE fell from $240,000 to roughly $196,000. The valuation dropped 20 percent accordingly.

She called me in tears. She had owned and operated this studio for nine years. She had been a model tenant—never late on rent, maintained the space meticulously, brought hundreds of people into a commercial corridor that was half-empty when she signed her original lease. And her landlord, protected by a lease that gave him full discretion over assignments, was holding her hostage.

What followed was two months of the most intense negotiation I've done. We brought in a commercial real estate attorney. We documented how much business the studio had brought to the neighborhood. We found comparable leases proving the demanded increase was well above market. We reminded the landlord that an empty space served no one. And—after multiple rounds of offers, counter-offers, and several moments we thought were the end—we landed at a 15 percent increase. Not sixty. Fifteen.

The deal closed. My client sold for $690,000—not the $720,000 we'd originally targeted, but not the $570,000 the landlord's opening demand would have dictated. Both buyers came back once the lease was resolved—a reminder that a clean assignment outcome can resurrect interest you thought was gone.

I share this story in full because the lesson isn't "landlords are villains." The lesson is: your lease is a legal document with financial consequences, and if you haven't read it recently, you don't know what it actually says. Most sellers don't.

One last lesson from the trenches: I once had a landlord demand 5 percent equity in the business as a condition of consenting to the lease assignment. It felt outrageous. But the business was worth it to the buyer, and after exploring every alternative, they agreed. That equity stake will cost the owner a meaningful sum when he eventually sells—money that would have stayed in his pocket if the lease assignment clause had been negotiated differently years earlier. Know what your lease actually says before a landlord uses it against you.

THE MOST IMPORTANT CLAUSE YOU'VE NEVER READ

Every commercial lease includes a provision governing what happens when the tenant wants to transfer the lease to another party. This is the assignment clause, and it determines how much leverage your landlord has when you try to sell.

Assignment clauses exist on a spectrum. At the seller-friendly end: "Tenant may assign this lease to any purchaser of substantially all of Tenant's business assets with Landlord's prior written consent, which shall not be unreasonably withheld." The super-friendly version comes with a full release of liability upon assignment.

At the landlord-friendly end: "Landlord may withhold consent to any assignment in Landlord's sole and absolute discretion." Translation: the landlord can block your sale for any reason at all. The difference between those two clauses is the difference between a landlord who can't block your sale and one who can demand 60 percent rent increases as a condition of consent.

Assignment clauses also commonly state that the seller will remain liable as a guarantor for the duration of the lease, including any renewal options. Nobody wants to be on the hook for a lease on a business they no longer own. But landlords want as many guarantors as they can get.

If your lease is at the landlord-friendly end of this spectrum and you have time before selling, try to negotiate better terms now—at lease renewal, or proactively as a lease amendment. A commercial real estate attorney who works with small business tenants can help you understand your leverage and how to use it.

THE RUNWAY BUYERS NEED

Buyers and lenders want certainty. They need to know they can operate the business long enough to recover their investment before facing a renewal negotiation or potentially having to move.

Buyers and SBA lenders generally want at least ten years of combined lease runway—meaning the remaining term plus renewal options added together. A lease with five years remaining and two five-year renewal options gives you fifteen total years—ideal. A lease with five years remaining and no renewal options is a harder story to tell, because hitting that ten-year threshold depends entirely on the land-lord's willingness to renew.

If your lease has less than three years remaining with no renewal options, you are in a more difficult position for a sale. Not an impossible one—but it's a real obstacle that will require your landlord's accommodation.

THE LIABILITY THAT FOLLOWS YOU OUT THE DOOR

Most commercial leases for small businesses require a personal guarantee—meaning you, the owner, are personally on the hook for rent even if the business can't pay. This is standard, and landlords are not going to waive it for new businesses.

At the time of a sale, the question becomes: Does your personal guarantee survive the sale? In most leases, yes—unless the landlord specifically releases you. This means that if the new owner fails to pay rent, you can still be held personally liable.

Negotiating a release of your personal guarantee should be an explicit item in your landlord consent negotiations. Some landlords will agree to release you once the new owner has established a track record—often after one year of on-time payments. Others won't, regardless of the new owner's payment history. Push for it, but don't assume you'll get it. And get any release in writing—have your attorney review the specific language.

THE THIRD PARTY WITH THEIR OWN AGENDA

Landlords who know and trust their tenants are far more cooperative in assignment negotiations than landlords who barely know who you are. If your interactions have been limited to signing checks, change that now—before you're in a sale. Be the tenant who makes the landlord's job easy. That goodwill is worth real money when it's time to negotiate your assignment. If you haven't read your assignment clause recently, do it this week. Everything else in this chapter flows from what it says.

If you own your building rather than lease it, you have a different set of options—sell the real estate with the business, keep the building and become the landlord, or sell the building separately. Each structure has different tax and buyer implications. See Appendix C for a full discussion of your options.

7

YOUR TEAM: THE REASON BUYERS SAY YES

The Austin yoga studio story showed what fear does to a deal. Here's what happens when buyers aren't afraid.

A client came to me with a Pilates studio that was performing well—good numbers, a good lease, a good location. What made it exceptional was the team. She had a general manager she'd been developing for three years, two lead instructors who had been with her since year one, and a front desk coordinator who had personally onboarded something like a thousand members.

When buyers toured the studio, they met these people. They saw what a business built on a team rather than a founder looked like. Three of the four offers we received mentioned the team specifically as a reason for their confidence. The business sold in sixty days at the high end of our target range. I've done transactions that took longer and generated more friction for businesses with objectively stronger financials because the human infrastructure wasn't in place.

THE ROLE THAT UNLOCKS YOUR EXIT

If you are currently the de facto general manager of your studio—if you're the one handling scheduling, managing operational issues, dealing with vendors, and making the day-to-day decisions that keep the business running—you need to hire someone to do that before you go to market.

This hire is not a cost. It is an investment in your sale price. A business with a qualified GM in place for twelve or more months commands a meaningfully higher multiple than the same business without one. Buyers can see the difference immediately: a business that runs when you're not there is a fundamentally different investment than one that requires your presence to function.

I know that for some of you, this hire feels out of reach—there are budget or timing considerations, or the right person hasn't appeared. That's okay. Even beginning to systematize and document your own role creates real value. The GM hire is the goal; moving in that direction is the first step.

What to look for in a GM hire: someone who can actually run the place, who loves the fitness world, who knows the software, and—most importantly—who can build real relationships with your staff and members. This person will be the face of your business during the transition, and their ability to maintain community trust matters as much as their operational competence.

WHAT HAPPENS WHEN YOUR BEST INSTRUCTOR LEAVES

Beyond the GM, buyers are evaluating your bench depth—the number of your instructors and staff who are ready to step up into bigger roles. Specifically: what happens if your most popular instructor leaves? Does the business survive? Does the membership churn? Or do you have two or three other instructors ready to step into that role?

The vacation test is a good proxy for bench depth. Could you take two weeks off—fully offline, not checking messages, not available for decisions—and come back to a business that ran normally in your absence? If the answer is yes, well done, you should do that more. If the answer is no, or if you'd admit it would be a stressful two weeks, you have work to do.

THE CONTRACTS THAT PROTECT EVERYONE

Key staff—your GM, your lead instructors, anyone whose departure would meaningfully affect the business—should be on written employment agreements that clearly define their roles, compensation structures, and basic policies. The compliance details—classification rules, handbook requirements, insurance—are covered in the next chapter.

The value side is just as important: when a buyer acquires your business, they can't count on the informal understanding you've built with your team. They need to see, on paper, what people are being paid and what their responsibilities are.

Non-solicitation clauses—which prevent departing staff from soliciting your members—are worth discussing with your attorney for key roles. Enforceability varies by state, so the specific language matters.

Written agreements, done well, formalize what already exists—and most employees prefer the clarity.

WHAT STAYING POWER SAYS ABOUT YOUR CULTURE

In a business where turnover is the norm—and in fitness, it often is—a stable, long-tenured team is a genuine differentiator. When buyers review your staff roster and see that your GM has been with you for three years, your lead instructor for five, and your front desk person for four—that's a signal about culture, management, and the environment you've built.

If your current tenure numbers are low—if you've had significant turnover in the past year—that's a story you'll need to be prepared to tell. Not defensively, but honestly. What changed? What did you learn from it? What does the team look like now? Buyers understand that turnover happens. What they're evaluating is whether you've addressed the underlying causes and won't miss a beat going forward.

WHEN TO TELL YOUR TEAM AND WHEN TO WAIT

You can tell your team both too early and too late. The timing is trickier than most people expect.

The standard guidance is consistent: don't tell the team until the deal is essentially done—documents signed, funds in transit. Tell them too early, and you introduce uncertainty at a vulnerable moment. Instructors start putting out feelers elsewhere. Members pick up on the anxiety. The morale cost can be real and measurable.

Key staff—particularly your GM—may need to know earlier. That conversation is worth having individually, carefully, and with the clear understanding that their confidence is required. Most long-tenured, trusted GMs handle this conversation well. They're professionals who care about you and the community, and this might be an opportunity for them as well.

When you have that conversation, be honest, be warm, and focus on what comes next for them. You're not abandoning them; you're handing the community they helped build to someone who can take it further. When it's framed that way, and introduced to a new owner who is visibly excited and respectful, it can be a celebration rather than a crisis.

I have a different take, though. I'm a huge advocate for making your staff aware of your intention to sell years in advance. Normalize it. Talk about it often. Make it not a big deal. A team that knows your intentions won't be surprised or afraid. They'll be prepared. And what I've seen consistently across dozens of deals is that the community makes the best buyers. The team you've built is your single greatest asset going into any sale. Protect it, develop it, and trust it to speak for itself.

8

YOUR GREATEST ASSET, YOUR GREATEST LIABILITY

I once worked with a studio owner who was certain she had always followed the rules—seven years, profitable, strong community. Then due diligence hit: five instructors classified as independent contractors who should have been employees. Back payroll taxes, penalties, and potential state liability. Her deal dropped $80,000 overnight, and she never saw it coming.

You met your team in the previous chapter—the reason buyers say yes. This chapter is the other side of that coin: the paper trail that proves you treated them right. Your employees will experience their own version of what you're going through. All of them deserve to know you treated them fairly, and a buyer's due diligence team will be reading the documentation of how you did that.

Buyers ask about HR not because they want to catch you in some gotcha. They ask because bad HR practices are expensive. Misclassified workers, informal arrangements, sloppy documentation—that's hidden cost. It either surfaces during due diligence, killing deal momentum or tanking the valuation, or it has to be fixed before closing.

EMPLOYEES OR CONTRACTORS: IT MATTERS

The number one HR mistake I see in boutique fitness is misclassification. Owners treat people as independent contractors, even though, under the law, they are actually employees.

The IRS has tests for this. State labor departments have their own, different tests. They all circle back to the same thing: control. Does the business control when, where, and how the work happens? Does the business provide the schedule, the studio, the members, and the equipment? Is the relationship ongoing, or is it a one-off project?

If you have instructors teaching your classes, in your space, on your schedule, to your members, those instructors are most likely employees under the law. The label on the contract doesn't matter. What matters is what would happen if you got audited.

California, like Massachusetts, has the ABC test, which is among the strictest in the country. Other states use a multi-factor test. The specifics vary. But the direction is the same: have this conversation with an employment attorney now. If you've been running on 1099 instructors and contractors, get clarity on who should be reclassified, when, and how.

The cost when a buyer finds a skeleton like this is brutal. Back taxes. Penalties. Statutory damages in some states. I've watched deals fall apart over misclassification. The buyer walks, demands a massive price cut, or demands you fix it before closing—which means retroactive payroll, back contributions, and difficult conversations with people who thought they were contractors and may not know you're selling.

The fix is simple. Do it now, before you're in deal mode and under pressure. Audit your classifications with your employment attorney and your CPA. Reclassify. Get proper payroll in place. The cost of fixing this proactively is nothing compared to the cost of getting caught unprepared.

WHAT YOUR HANDBOOK SAYS ABOUT YOU

In the early years, many fitness studios run on relationships and hand-shake agreements. The owner shrugs about PTO and says, "Whatever, enjoy Burning Man." Rules and expectations may or may not exist, and if they do, they live in the owner's head or a random text thread.

Everyone understands if you're just starting. But no one understands it when you're trying to sell. A buyer is acquiring a business that they can't run on your institutional memory. They need to know: what's the PTO policy? How much sick leave does each employee have? What's the protocol for covering a class? What happens if someone gets injured? All of that needs to be documented, in writing, and consistently communicated to the team.

Here's the thing that surprises most owners: more than twenty states now have mandatory paid sick leave laws. Some cities, too. The requirements are all different. Some states say "three days." Some say "five." Some have different rules for part-time versus full-time. And this list keeps growing.

You need an employment attorney to map out your state's requirements and any city ordinances that apply to you. Then, write a policy that meets or exceeds those requirements. Communicate it to your team. Document that communication. One week of work. Done. And when a buyer asks if you're compliant with paid sick leave laws, you hand them a folder with the policy and proof you've been following it.

ARE YOU PROPERLY COVERED?

One more thing buyers will ask for: your insurance certificates: workers' comp, general liability, the works. Make sure the coverage is current, adequate, and actually covers the specific activities you run. I've seen policies with carve-outs for things like aerial yoga or reformer classes that the owner never noticed. Any lapse or gap between what you think is covered and what actually is creates problems during due diligence.

FIX IT BEFORE BUYERS FIND IT

I know "HR audit" sounds like the most boring thing in this book, but it's worth it: get one before you go to market. Hire an employment attorney or an HR consultant who works with small businesses. They'll spend a day or two with you, reviewing your classifications, handbook, policies, insurance, and payroll records. They'll identify what's missing. You fix it. You have documentation of the audit and the fixes.

A year before you plan to sell is the right time. You're not under pressure. You have time to make changes without rushing. When a buyer's attorney asks about HR practices in due diligence, you hand them a folder. Clean records. Compliant classifications. Written policies. Professional audit. It reduces buyer risk. It reduces negotiating friction. It reduces the chance that something emerges in due diligence that blows up a deal you've spent months building.

Every person on your team deserves your attention to this. Getting it right honors them and helps ease any remnants of guilt you might be feeling.

9

PLANTING SEEDS: YOUR BEST BUYERS ARE ALREADY IN CLASS

Most sellers imagine that selling a business works like listing a house: you put it on the market, buyers show up, and you pick the best one. There's some truth to that. But the deals I'm most proud of—the ones that close fastest, at the highest prices, with the cleanest terms—almost never came entirely from strangers who found a listing online.

They came from seeds planted long before the business officially went to market.

The concept is simple: your best buyer is likely already in your orbit. They could be a current employee, a member, a competitor who knows your business, or a local entrepreneur who's admired what you've built for years. These people don't need to be convinced your business is a good investment—they already believe it. The trust is already there.

All you have to do is make them aware of the opportunity—even years in advance, even just a casual mention: "I've been thinking about my next chapter when my kids go to college next year, and I think you'd be an ideal person to take on my business. Let me know if you are interested or ever want to talk about it."

That's it. That's all you have to say.

Everyone hearing this takes it as a huge compliment. Much like inviting someone to a teacher training, they are flattered.

"Me?! You think I'd be an ideal person?"

That seed gets planted, and the person begins the mental journey at their own pace—sometimes surfacing months later, sometimes years. When they do come back, both parties show up emotionally prepared. The trust and familiarity are already there, and when you pair that with real competition from outside buyers, these internal candidates almost always come out on top.

THE BUYER WHO ALREADY LOVES YOUR BUSINESS

There's a common fear among sellers about talking to internal candidates. What if they get spooked? What if word gets out before you're ready? What if your best employee suddenly feels uncertain and starts looking for another job?

These fears are legitimate, and I'm not suggesting you call a staff meeting and announce you're selling. What I am suggesting is that you start having more intentional conversations with people who might be interested—long before you're officially in the process.

The best version of this is a general manager you've been developing for years. You've given them ownership of the operational day-to-day. They've seen the financials, or at least the performance metrics. They understand what makes the business work. They love the clients, and the staff trusts them. When the time comes to talk about the future of the business, they're not shocked—they're already thinking about it. And in some cases, they're the best buyer you could find, because they know exactly what they're getting and they're already invested in the outcome.

Employee acquisitions funded through SBA loans are increasingly common in our industry. A qualified GM with good credit and a compelling business case can absolutely purchase the business they've been helping run. I've closed several of these, and they tend to be among the smoothest closes I've ever done—because the buyer already knows the business, the staff knows and trusts the buyer, and the transition is natural.

PLANTING SEEDS WITHOUT TIPPING YOUR HAND

Beyond your internal team, your professional network is a source of buyers that most sellers dramatically overlook.

Think about who's in your professional orbit: multi-unit operators in your franchise system looking to expand, real estate investors who want an operating business to pair with a space, entrepreneurs in adjacent industries, members who've mentioned wanting to do something entrepreneurial, and former instructors who've opened their own spaces and might want a second location.

I advise sellers to start having what I call soft conversations—not " I'm selling, are you interested?" but rather "I've been thinking about the long-term future of the business and what ownership transition might look like. Would you be interested in a conversation about that someday?" You'd be surprised how many times someone says, "Actually, I've thought about that too."

The key is to actually believe it's not a big deal—because it isn't. If you're relaxed about it, the other person will be too. If you're sweating and anxious, people will think something is wrong. Of course you're going to sell your business someday. The more you talk about it between now and then, the less scary it becomes for everyone.

WHO YOUR BUYERS ACTUALLY ARE

When I go to market with a business, I'm reaching across several different buyer categories simultaneously.

Individual owner-operators are the most common buyers in our industry—typically someone leaving corporate life or a fitness professional stepping into ownership. They often use SBA loans, which means they need to qualify and that the deal must conform to SBA guidelines (see Chapter Nineteen). They move thoughtfully, sometimes slowly, but they're often ideal because they're deeply invested in the mission.

Serial entrepreneurs already own businesses and are looking to add to their portfolios. They move faster, understand financials, and often have capital ready. Private equity and strategic buyers are increasingly present, particularly for businesses with multiple locations or unique IP. These conversations take longer, but the outcomes can be extraordinary—especially if you've been building the relationship for years before the sale.

TURNING NAMES INTO CONVERSATIONS

As you build your list of potential buyers over the months and years before your sale, keep it organized and keep the relationships warm. When the time comes to go to market, the difference between a cold approach and a warm network is often measured in months and hundreds of thousands of dollars.

10

SELL AT YOUR PEAK

People love to ask about the market. When is the right time to sell? Is the market good right now? Should I wait?

The biggest timing mistake I see isn't selling too early or too late. It's waiting until something forces the issue. Family crises, health problems, landlord conflicts, staff departures—the instructor who goes down the street and starts competing with you, which is painfully common in our industry. Fires, hurricanes, social unrest. We've seen it all.

The best time to sell is when everything is going great. If your business is running the smoothest it's ever been, and you don't think it'll get better than this—that's the moment. Because when something bad goes down, the multiples follow.

IT'S NOT ABOUT THE MARKET

When sellers ask me about timing, they're usually thinking about external market conditions—interest rates, the economy, and whether boutique fitness is trending. These things matter at the margins, but they're rarely the primary driver of whether a deal gets done and at what price.

What matters far more is your personal readiness. Are you ready to move on? Are your financials clean and verifiable? Is your management team in place? Is your lease solid? Is the business growing or at least stable? If all of those things are true, you're in a good position to sell regardless of what the broader market is doing. If any of them are broken, no amount of favorable market conditions will save you.

That said, there are specific windows in your own studio's business cycle that make more sense than others. The best time to go to market is typically when you've just completed a strong year. A buyer needs to believe in the business's future, and a recent strong year gives them that confidence. A recent down year, even if it was an anomaly, raises questions that take months to answer and may kill deals entirely.

ONE HARD RULE ABOUT TIMING

Give yourself at least one full year of intentional exit preparation. Two is better. Three is ideal.

Two years gives you enough runway to work through every preparation step covered in Part One—clean financials, a trained GM, a favorable lease, a growing membership base, and a pipeline of interested buyers. Rush it, and you leave money on the table or scramble through due diligence.

SEASONALITY AND THE VALUATION WINDOW

Boutique fitness is one of the most seasonal businesses in the consumer economy. January is not July. A cycle studio in a college town loses a third of its active members every May and rebuilds in September. A yoga studio in a beach community spikes in summer and flattens in winter. A Lagree studio crests in the new year and softens by March. If you've been running your business for more than two years, you already know your seasonal pattern in your bones. What you may not have thought about is how that pattern affects your valuation, your due diligence, and the story a buyer's lender will tell about your numbers.

SDE is calculated on trailing twelve-month revenue—meaning the window you choose matters. A studio that went to market in January, when Q4 memberships were at their annual low, is presenting a different trailing number than one that went to market in March, after the new-year surge had run its course. Neither is dishonest. Both are real. But the timing affects what buyers see first and what questions they ask.

The practical guidance: choose your go-to-market timing deliberately. If your strongest revenue months are January through March, going to market in April lets those months anchor your trailing twelve. The goal is to show your business at its structural best, not just its statistical peak.

Annotate your monthly P&L for seasonality before presenting it to buyers. A single column of notes—"annual July dip due to summer break" or "Q1 spike reflects January teacher training cycle"—is far better than leaving a buyer's accountant to flag the variation as unexplained. Unexplained variation triggers questions and extends timelines. Explained variation is just context. Give them the context.

One more thing worth knowing: SBA lenders underwrite on debt service coverage, meaning they care whether the business generates enough cash flow each month to cover the loan payment. A studio with three months a year when cash flow dips below the coverage threshold—even if the annual average is strong—can create a financing challenge. You need to be able to speak to seasonality with confidence.

SOMETIMES THE ANSWER IS "NOT YET"

Sometimes the answer is "Not yet." And I will always tell a client the truth about that, even when it's not what they want to hear.

You probably need more time if: your books are a mess, and a buyer's accountant would spend more time asking questions than evaluating the business. Your general manager is new, or the role doesn't exist yet. Your lease expires in less than three years with no renewal options. Your revenue is declining, and there's no clear turnaround story. Or your business is too personally tied to you, and you haven't built the systems or team to operate without you.

None of these is permanent. Most can be fixed in twelve to twenty-four months. But start now.

11

IF NOW IS THE TIME

The previous chapter assumed you're selling from a position of strength, with time on your side. This one is for everyone else —the owners who don't have the luxury of waiting or rebuilding. Your options are fewer, but they're not gone. What matters now is honesty about where you stand and clarity about what comes next.

IF YOU'RE ALREADY IN DECLINE: YOUR REAL OPTIONS

Oftentimes, an honest assessment is exactly what you need to move forward.

First, no judgment here. Numbers are what they are. But understand what declining numbers actually do to your valuation. SDE is typically calculated as a weighted average of the trailing two to three years, with most weight given to the most recent year. A business that earned $300,000 three years ago, $240,000 two years ago, and $180,000 last year will have its SDE calculated closer to $180,000 than $300,000—and a buyer will apply a lower multiple on top of that, because declining trends signal risk. The double compression of lower earnings and lower multiple is what makes distressed sales so painful. A business that might have sold for $1.2 million at its peak may realistically sell for $400,000 to $500,000 on a declining trajectory.

Second, understand your actual options—roughly in order of likely outcome:

Stabilize, then sell. If the decline is addressable—a staffing problem, a marketing gap, a lease renegotiation, a specific operational issue—and you have the energy and resources, fix it. A twelve-month turnaround that stops the bleeding and shows a flat or recovering trend line can meaningfully improve your outcome. You don't need to return to the peak. You need to show that the trend has reversed. Buyers buy stories about the future, not autopsies of the past.

Sell now, honestly priced. If you don't have the energy or the capital for a turnaround, the worst thing you can do is price the business at what it was worth two years ago and sit on the market for eighteen months while it continues to decline. Price it at what it's worth now, be transparent about the trend, and find a buyer who sees the turnaround opportunity and has the resources to execute it. Turnaround buyers exist. They typically pay less—sometimes significantly less—but a deal at a lower price is infinitely better than no deal at all.

Wind down intentionally. Sometimes the honest answer is that the business isn't sellable at a price that makes the effort worthwhile—particularly if the lease is short, the equipment is aged, and the membership base has shrunk below a critical threshold. A thoughtful wind-down—giving members time to transition, honoring your team, and negotiating an early lease termination—is a legitimate outcome that preserves your reputation and relationships, even when the financials are disappointing.

Whatever situation you're in, being honest with yourself and your advisors is the most important thing. The sellers I've watched get hurt the worst are the ones who spent two years refusing to acknowledge the trajectory, making things significantly worse before finally facing reality. The sooner you know where you stand, the sooner you can choose the right path.

SELL WHILE YOU STILL LOVE IT

Another issue I see often: sellers who are waiting for the right moment that will never come. They want the business to be just a little bit more profitable, just a little more systematized, just a little bigger. And in their waiting, they grind themselves down past the point where they have the energy to do it well.

Here's a counterintuitive truth: the best sellers are the ones who still love what they do. They have energy. They can talk about the business with genuine enthusiasm, and that enthusiasm transfers to buyers. Buyers can tell the difference between an owner who's still excited about what they've built and doesn't need to sell at all, and one who's exhausted and wants out. The first one gets premium offers. The second one does not.

If you find yourself dreading Mondays, fantasizing about what you'd do if you didn't have to run this business, snapping at your staff, or taking calls from members with an impatience you never used to feel —pay attention to those signals. The best exit is one you make from a position of strength, before you burn out entirely.

THE PAUSE THAT EARNED $140,000

One client called us in the spring—a CrossFit-adjacent strength studio owner in the Mountain West—and told us he'd started his process with his preferred buyer at a clear number: $850,000. That was his number. He'd communicated it to his buyer, believed in it, and intended to hold it. But that was six months ago. Now, after months of grinding with a single buyer who kept slowing down the process, revising his offer, adding document requests, and then going quiet for weeks at a time, my client was mentally at $680,000 and falling. He hadn't moved the number in any conversation. The buyer hadn't had to ask him to move it. But the exhaustion of a single-buyer process had done the work for him.

I looked at his financials. The valuation was supportable, but there were two problems: one year of tax returns didn't match the prior year's

P&L methodology, and he'd never hired and trained a proper GM, so the business was showing as owner-dependent. These weren't fatal issues, but they were exactly the kind of things a single buyer with time on his side could use against you forever.

I recommended he pause the process. Take six months, fix the discrepancy with his CPA, hire and orient a GM, and come back to market with a cleaner story and a wider buyer pool. He agreed—reluctantly, because he was exhausted and wanted to be done.

When we went to market six months later with those issues resolved, we had three offers within eight weeks. He sold for $820,000 to a buyer he chose because she had the best plan for the community—not because she was the only one at the table. That pause took him six months. It both made the sale possible and earned him an extra $140,000.

PART II

GOING TO MARKET

12

EVERYONE NEEDS A SPECIALIST

Obviously, I have a vested interest in you reading this book and concluding that you should engage Boutique Fitness Broker to help sell your business. That's worth acknowledging. But now that it's acknowledged, let me tell you why I think every business should be sold by a broker who specializes in their industry.

A good broker understands you, your business, and your industry well enough to differentiate your business from every other. The details matter. You don't want someone oblivious to the differences between classical and contemporary Pilates if they're selling a Pilates studio. The reputation of a studio's teacher training, the specifics of the equipment, the certifying bodies, and the intellectual property—buyers will ask about all of it, and the broker needs to address these issues as articulately as the owner.

There's also the question of fit. Maybe the seller is great at sales, and the buyer is great at marketing. A specialist broker can spot that, recommend the right consultants, log into the CRM and walk a buyer through the reporting, and give real confidence that the operation won't fall apart after the transition.

Most importantly, a good broker means you walk away with more money, even after the fees. The right preparation, the right asking price, and the execution of the sale process get you there. Added bonus: they'll run the whole process for you from start to finish and be your best friend and confidant the whole time.

In more than seventy transactions, I've seen what good brokerage does for these deals, and I've heard what the absence of it does. We have an 80 percent close rate. The industry average is far lower. I want every business owner to have someone equally invested in their industry guiding them through a process they've likely never experienced before and never will again.

MORE THAN JUST A LISTING AGENT

A business broker helps you price the business, prepares marketing materials, finds and vets buyers, manages the process, and earns a fee at closing—usually between 8 and 12 percent for smaller transactions, with lower percentages on larger deals. Sometimes there's a small listing fee upfront to ensure both parties are fully committed.

The comparison to real estate agents is tempting but breaks down fast. Selling a business means managing a financial narrative, a human infrastructure, a lease, a customer base, an operational dependency on the owner, and a hundred other variables that have to be communicated, verified, and negotiated. A good broker positions all of that for maximum clarity, manages the emotional dynamics on both sides, and gets the deal across the finish line when it hits turbulence.

THE BROKER AND THE ATTORNEY: WHO DOES WHAT

First-time sellers are often confused about how a business broker and an M&A attorney work together. It's a fair question—both are involved in every deal and neither fully explains the other's role.

The broker's job is the front half of the transaction: valuation, marketing, finding and vetting buyers, managing the process, and negotiating the key commercial terms—price, structure, timeline. The broker is your guide through the market and your advocate at the table.

When you have three offers and need to decide which to accept and what to counter, that conversation happens with your broker.

The attorney's job is the back half: drafting and negotiating the legal documents that convert the agreed commercial terms into binding obligations. The Letter of Intent, the Purchase Agreement, the Bill of Sale, the non-compete, the reps and warranties—all of this is the attorney's domain. When the buyer's counsel sends over a purchase agreement with favorable-to-buyer language buried in a definition on page thirty-four, your attorney is the one who finds it and pushes back.

In practice, the two work in parallel through the middle of the transaction—the broker manages the commercial negotiation while the attorney handles the legal documentation. They should be communicating with each other, not just with you. A deal with a good broker and no experienced attorney is one in which the seller's interests are exposed at the most legally consequential moment. A deal that has a good attorney and no broker often never gets to market, or gets there underprepared.

When seeking an M&A attorney, look for someone who has closed business sale transactions, not just general contract work. Ask specifically how many asset purchase agreements they've drafted in the last two years and what the deal sizes were. A real estate attorney, a family law attorney, or heaven forbid a divorce attorney can all draft legal documents—but the specific mechanics of a small business asset sale, including holdback structures, rep and warranty negotiation, and SBA-compliant documentation, require someone who lives in this space. The cost of a good M&A attorney is a fraction of what bad documentation can cost you after closing.

THE QUESTIONS TO ASK BEFORE YOU SIGN

The brokerage industry has a quality problem. Licensing requirements vary by state, many brokers are part-time or generalists, and a generalist who sold a laundromat last month will have no relationships with fitness business buyers, no framework for valuing membership-based recurring revenue, and no understanding of instructor classification, teacher trainings, or membership transfers. The business sits on the market, the seller gets discouraged, and a deal that should have happened doesn't. So vet your broker carefully.

When you're evaluating a broker, ask specific questions. How many boutique fitness businesses have you sold in the last two years? What were the sale prices relative to the asking prices? What's your close rate —meaning, of the businesses you list, what percentage actually sell? How do you find buyers? What does your marketing process look like? How do you handle confidentiality during the listing period?

You want a broker who can speak specifically and fluently about your type of business, who has actual relationships with buyers in your category, whose close rate is meaningfully above the industry average, and who makes you feel like a partner in the process rather than a transaction.

Find a broker who will tell you the truth about the right asking price, even if that truth is uncomfortable. The brokers who inflate valuation expectations to win the listing and then spend the next year walking you down to reality are doing you a disservice. A broker who gives you an honest number on day one—and then explains what you can do to increase it—is worth far more than one who tells you what you want to hear.

Most reputable brokers will ask for an exclusive listing agreement, typically for six to twelve months. This is standard and reasonable. It takes real time and money to do this right, and a broker can only afford to do that if they know they'll have the chance to earn their fee.

Read the agreement carefully, particularly around the commission structure and what happens if it doesn't work out. Look at the exit clauses. If the broker isn't performing—not generating interest, not providing regular updates—you want a clear path to terminate the relationship without penalty.

THE ONE TIME YOU MIGHT NOT NEED ONE

If you already have a strong, specific buyer who is ready, willing, and able to give you everything you want—and who was not found through a broker's marketing efforts—you may not need a broker to manage the transaction. You will still need an attorney to draft and review the Purchase Agreement, and you should have an accountant verify your financials.

But even in that scenario, I'd encourage you to consult with a broker before finalizing anything—not to hire them for the full transaction, but to get an outside opinion on whether the price is fair and whether other buyers might compete. Even knowing what the market might pay changes your negotiating position with the buyer in front of you.

13

KEEPING IT A SECRET

Every year, owners come to me because someone approached them out of nowhere. A competitor made an inquiry. A private equity group sent a letter. A member mentioned they'd been looking to buy a studio. What do you do when a buyer finds you before you're ready?

First: Don't say yes or no to anything. Listen, ask questions, and express genuine interest in continuing the conversation—without making any commitments or disclosing any financial information. The instinct is either to get excited and start talking numbers or to shut it down because you're not ready. Both are mistakes.

Second: Understand that an unsolicited offer is almost always below what you'd get in a competitive process. The buyer found you specifically because they believe they can acquire your business without competition. That's the condition that drives prices down.

Third: Treat it as a signal, not a transaction. If one buyer found you compelling, others likely will too. Use the interest as a catalyst to get your preparation in order and run a real market process. Get your broker involved before you go further—walking into even an informal negotiation without representation is one of the most common and costly mistakes I see.

Going to market is one of the most nerve-wracking parts of this entire process, and the reason is almost always the same: you're terrified of someone finding out.

Your staff might hear and start looking for other jobs. Your members might get anxious and cancel. Your competitors might try to poach your clients. Your landlord might get spooked. All of these fears are valid, and managing confidentiality well is one of the things I take most seriously.

HOW WE KEEP YOU PROTECTED

Here's how we manage it. The business goes to market without being publicly identified. The listing describes the business in general terms —"Established boutique fitness studio in a major metropolitan area, ten-plus years in operation, 400+ active members, strong recurring revenue"—without naming the studio, the city (sometimes), or any identifying details.

When a buyer expresses interest, they sign a Non-Disclosure Agreement before receiving any specific information. Only after the NDA is signed do they learn the name of the business, its location, and the financial details. This protects you from competitors who might inquire just to snoop, from casual browsers who aren't serious, and from anyone who might share the information carelessly.

Once a serious buyer is engaged, the flow of information is controlled carefully—one step at a time.

THE SECRET YOU HAVE TO KEEP FROM YOUR OWN PEOPLE

The external confidentiality framework handles what the market knows. The harder challenge—the one that keeps most sellers up at night—is internal: managing the secret from your own people.

For most sellers, the team represents the most acute emotional exposure in the entire process. Your general manager, your lead instructors, your front desk person who knows every member by name

—these are people you've worked alongside for years, some of them your closest professional relationships. And throughout the sale process, you are withholding something significant from all of them.

There is no way to make this easy. What I can offer is guidance to help manage it.

If you read Chapter Seven and took my advice about normalizing the idea of selling over time—talking openly with your team about your long-term plans, planting seeds with potential buyers years in advance—you might be wondering why this chapter tells you to keep everything a secret. The distinction matters. Chapter Seven is the long game: creating a culture where your eventual exit isn't a shock. This chapter is the short game: protecting your team, your members, and your deal from unnecessary anxiety once the formal sale process is live. Telling your GM two years ago that you plan to sell someday is not the same as telling them you signed an LOI last Tuesday. Both conversations are important. They serve completely different purposes.

The Planting Seeds conversations from Chapter Nine don't stop—those are about cultivating buyers, not disclosing a live deal. What changes here is how tightly you control information once the process is real and the stakes are immediate.

First: Don't tell anyone on your team until the deal is materially done—meaning a Purchase Agreement is signed, the Lease Assignment is approved, and the deal is set to close. Not your most trusted manager. Not the instructor who has been with you for eight years. This isn't a question of trust. It's that putting someone in the position of carrying that secret is unfair to them. The anxiety it creates in them tends to telegraph to other staff and members before you're ready, in ways neither of you intends.

One important exception: if someone on your team is in your buyer pool—a manager who has expressed genuine interest in ownership, for example—that relationship is handled differently. As we discuss in Chapter Nine, those conversations are exploratory and individual, structured to let you step back gracefully if the deal doesn't materialize. That's a different situation from general staff disclosure, and it gets treated as one.

Second: People may notice something is different. You may have more closed-door calls than usual. You may seem preoccupied. My guidance is to prepare a brief, honest, non-specific answer for the "Is everything okay?" conversation that will eventually come. Something like: "All is well! I'm working on some new things. Nothing that affects the team—I'll be able to share more soon." That is not a lie. It is, in every meaningful sense, the truth.

Third: The moment a deal moves into closing, tell your key people before it becomes public in any other way. They deserve to hear it from you, directly, before they hear it from anyone else. I'll cover exactly how to have that conversation in Chapter Twenty-One.

The stretch between deciding to sell and actually closing is one of the loneliest periods most sellers experience. You are living two lives simultaneously—outwardly, you're still the owner, still teaching, still greeting members, still posting on Instagram like everything is normal, while inwardly, you've already begun to let go. That split is exhausting, and some sellers describe a strange guilt about showing up fully for people while privately working toward the day they'll leave them. If you feel this way, it doesn't mean you're doing anything wrong. It means you care. The sellers who handle it best are the ones who have a small, trusted circle outside the business—a partner, a close friend, a mentor—who can hold the real conversation when the professional world can't. Build that circle before you start the process.

14

TELLING YOUR STORY AND
FINDING THE RIGHT BUYER

The primary marketing document for your business is called an offering memorandum or a confidential information memorandum (CIM). Think of it as the business equivalent of a listing brochure, except instead of photos of the kitchen, it contains a narrative about the business, three to five years of financial history, market analysis, and key operational details.

A well-written CIM tells the story of your business. Not just the numbers, but the opportunity—why this business, in this market, at this moment, represents a compelling investment. It anticipates and answers the questions a sophisticated buyer will ask. It's honest about challenges and transparent about risks, because experienced buyers can sniff out a one-sided pitch, and they're immediately skeptical when a business looks too perfect.

The financial section is where buyers form their first real impression of the business—and where deals are won or lost before a single conversation happens. This is where your Seller's Discretionary Earnings are laid out, your addbacks explained and documented, your membership trends and revenue breakdown presented clearly. (See Appendix B for a glossary of key financial terms.) A CIM with messy financials or unexplained variances signals that the business itself is messy.

WHY CORRECT BEATS OPTIMISTIC EVERY TIME

Setting the asking price is more art than science, but there's a framework. I start with the SDE calculation—three years of adjusted earnings, weighted toward the most recent year. Then I apply a market multiple that reflects the business's size, stability, growth trajectory, and risk profile, and check that number against comparable sales in the market.

I generally recommend pricing your business correctly, not leaving "room to negotiate." Overpricing kills deals—a buyer who sees an asking price disconnected from any reasonable valuation simply moves on. Pricing correctly invites interest. It signals that you've done your homework, gives you room to move without capitulating, and creates competition.

HOW WE FIND YOUR PERFECT BUYER

With your CIM prepared and your pricing set, we begin outreach simultaneously across several channels. Warm network first: the seeds you've been planting over the past year or two. Then, online business marketplaces like BizBuySell and BusinessBroker.net. Social media and emails to our personal list of thousands of buyers. Industry networks—conferences, trade associations, franchisor networks. And finally, targeted direct outreach for businesses with unique characteristics or higher value.

THE BUYER MEETING IS A TWO-WAY INTERVIEW

First conversations with buyers are always exploratory—chemistry checks as much as anything else. Does this person understand the industry? Do they have realistic expectations? Are they financially qualified? Are they someone you'd be comfortable handing your community to?

Yes, that last one matters. This isn't just a financial transaction. You built a community, and that community trusts you. A buyer who is excited about the mission—who asks about the members, who wants to understand the culture, who seems to care about the people involved —will be a far better steward of what you've built than someone who's just running the numbers.

Trust your gut in these early conversations. Deals can be killed or saved by chemistry before a single number is negotiated.

WHAT MAKES A GREAT BUYER

Chemistry matters, but gut feel alone isn't enough. Over the years, I've developed a clearer sense of what separates the buyers who become great stewards from those who looked good on paper but weren't. Here's what I actually watch for.

They ask about the people before they ask about the numbers. A buyer who opens the conversation with questions about your members, your team, the culture you've built—before asking about revenue multiples or lease terms—is telling you something important about how they see the business. They understand that the numbers follow the community, not the other way around. The buyer who leads with "What's your monthly churn rate?" is acquiring a financial asset. The buyer who leads with "How did you build such a loyal membership?" is acquiring your life's work. Those are different people.

They have a specific plan, not just enthusiasm. Enthusiasm is easy. Anyone can tell you they love fitness and have always dreamed of owning a studio. What you want to hear is something specific—what they would change, what they would keep, which modality they want to add, how they'd develop the team. Specificity signals that they've given serious thought to the business rather than just the idea of owning it. A buyer with a real plan is also less likely to freeze when something unexpected happens in the first year.

They're honest about what they don't know. The most dangerous buyer isn't the one who has never run a fitness business—it's the one who has never run a fitness business and doesn't know it. A buyer who says, "I've been in corporate for twenty years, I don't know this world yet, but I'm committed to learning it," is showing you self-awareness. That person will ask for help, respect the transition period, and not assume they know better than your team on day one.

They understand that they're not just buying a business—they're inheriting a trust. The best buyers I've worked with have said, in some form, "I understand that the members trusted you, and now they'll have to decide whether to trust me." When you hear that, pay attention. That's the buyer worth choosing, even if someone else offers more money.

WHAT THE BUYER IS GOING THROUGH

One thing worth remembering as you enter this phase: every serious buyer is carrying their own version of the anxiety you're feeling. They're about to hand over the largest check they've ever written for something they can't fully understand until they own it. When a buyer asks the same question a third time, they're not being difficult—they're scared. The sellers who close the best deals are those who can hold their own anxiety and still show empathy for the buyers.

15

WHY ONE BUYER IS RARELY ENOUGH

A buyer who believes they're competing for your business behaves completely differently from a buyer who believes they're the only option. They move faster, offer more, and are less likely to make unreasonable requests. When problems arise, they're motivated to work through them—because walking away means losing to someone else.

A buyer who believes they're the only one at the table does the opposite. They drag things out, probe for weaknesses, and offer less than they'd otherwise pay. When something comes up in due diligence—and something always does—they use it to renegotiate downward.

Remember the Introduction—the seller who spent twelve months with a single buyer and kept $600,000 more once a competing offer appeared? That's what competition does. One additional buyer at the table changes everything.

THE ANATOMY OF YOUR TRANSACTION

Many business transactions in the $500,000 to $5,000,000 range are financed through the SBA 7(a) loan program. Buyers can acquire businesses with as little as 10 percent down, with the remaining amount financed by a bank with a government guarantee. In a standard SBA transaction with no seller note requirement, the entire purchase price gets paid to you at closing in cash. If the deal requires a seller note—as some SBA transactions do—a portion of it comes to you over time, which we cover in the seller note section of Chapter Nineteen.

As we covered in Chapter Four, SBA deals have a practical ceiling of roughly 3x to 3.5x SDE. Above that, you'll need extra cash or creative financing.

Competition bridges that gap. When SBA-backed buyers and cash buyers compete simultaneously, each pushes past their floor price to stay in the game. The SBA ceiling is a real constraint on individual transactions—but competition among buyers with different financing capacity is how sellers break through it entirely.

NEGOTIATE FROM STRENGTH, NOT DESPERATION

Here's what I try to communicate to every seller I work with as they enter the negotiation phase: your goal is not to win. Your goal is for both of you to be okay with it.

A buyer who feels like they got a fair deal—who feels respected in the process, whose concerns were heard, whose reasonable requests were accommodated—becomes a steward who will take care of your business. A buyer who feels like they got squeezed, who had to fight for every concession, who felt like the seller was hiding things or playing games, starts the next chapter of ownership with resentment. And resentment makes everything harder: the transition, the staff relationships, the landlord relationship, the banking relationship.

Pursue your maximum outcome in a way that leaves the buyer feeling good about what they paid for it. Those things can coexist, and they should.

MANAGING COMPETING OFFERS: WHAT ACTUALLY WORKS

Competition is your strongest position. But most sellers who have multiple offers for the first time don't know how to manage them.

Don't reveal the specific terms of one offer to another buyer. If you have genuine competing offers, make sure each buyer knows it—real competition is already your strongest card, and you don't need to manufacture the appearance of it. But sharing specific numbers or terms from another LOI is both unprofessional and potentially a breach of confidentiality. When competition is real, the right way to communicate it is simply: "We have multiple serious offers, and we expect to make a decision by Friday. If you want to be in the final consideration, now is the time to put your best terms forward." Let serious buyers determine their own best offer rather than being anchored by a competitor's specific terms.

Compare offers on total value, not headline price. A $1,100,000 offer with a 20 percent holdback, a two-year earnout, and a ninety-day due diligence period may be worth less to you than a $900,000 all-cash offer with a 5 percent holdback and a thirty-day close. Build a simple side-by-side: net proceeds at closing, holdback amount and period, earnout exposure, financing contingency risk, and buyer qualification. The number that matters is what you'll actually receive and when—not what's at the top of the LOI.

Give each buyer a deadline, not a window. "Let me know whenever you're ready" invites delay. "We need final offers by Thursday at five" creates a forcing function. Serious buyers will meet your deadline. Buyers who miss it are telling you something about how they'll behave in due diligence and closing. Respect that information.

When a buyer demands an answer before the others are in, hold your position. This is a pressure tactic, and a common one. A buyer who says "I need a decision today or I'm out" before your process is complete is almost never actually out—they're testing your resolve. The right answer: "We're running a defined process, and we respect your timeline. If our process doesn't work for you, we understand, but we're not in a position to shortcut it." A buyer who genuinely walks over a reasonable two-day extension was never your buyer.

When offers are within 10 percent of each other, choose the one that fits. The buyer's plan for the business, their respect for your team, their communication style during the process—that's the right tiebreaker.

16

FROM LOI TO EXCLUSIVITY

When a buyer gets serious, they'll submit a Letter of Intent —an LOI. This is a non-binding document that outlines the key terms of the proposed deal: purchase price, deal structure, proposed due diligence period, closing timeline, and key conditions.

"Non-binding" is important to understand. An LOI is not a contract. What it is, practically speaking, is a signal of seriousness and a framework for negotiation. Once you sign an LOI with a buyer, you're typically entering an exclusive period with them—you've taken the business off the market, and you're focused on making this specific deal work.

Which is why the LOI stage is exactly where having multiple offers matters most. If you have three buyers who've submitted LOIs, you have choices. You can compare not just price but terms. A higher purchase price paid partly in seller financing over five years is worth less than a lower purchase price paid all cash at closing. (See Appendix B for definitions of earnouts, seller notes, and other deal structure terms.)

WHAT TO NEGOTIATE BEFORE YOU SIGN THE LOI

Most sellers treat the LOI as the beginning of the negotiation. Experienced sellers know it's the end of their peak leverage. Once you sign and enter exclusivity, the buyer knows you're off the market. The urgency that drove their offer softens. Their attorney gets involved. The process slows. Which means the LOI itself is the moment to negotiate—not just the price, but the terms that will govern everything that follows.

LOIs are usually drafted by the buyer's attorney, which means the defaults favor the buyer. Here are the specific points worth pushing back on before you sign.

The due diligence period length: Most LOIs propose thirty to sixty days. Sixty is generous to a buyer; it gives them time to drag out the process, find objections, and wear you down. Thirty days is sufficient for a well-prepared seller with a data room ready. Push for the shortest period your preparation can support. Every extra week of exclusivity is a week the business is off the market.

What happens if the buyer walks: The LOI should specify under what conditions the buyer can exit without consequence—and what, if anything, happens if they walk for reasons that aren't genuine due diligence findings. Some LOIs include a break fee paid to the seller if the buyer terminates without cause after a certain point. This isn't common in small-business transactions, but it's worth understanding whether your LOI provides any protection here at all.

The exclusivity carve-outs: Standard exclusivity prevents you from marketing the business or negotiating with other buyers. Make sure your LOI specifies what can terminate the exclusivity—specifically, what constitutes a material change that lets you exit and go back to market. A buyer who changes the deal terms significantly after signing—reducing the price, changing the structure, adding onerous conditions—should not be able to hold you in exclusivity indefinitely. But that protection only exists if your LOI explicitly says so—it must be negotiated and written in before you sign.

The holdback structure: If the LOI references a holdback, the percentage and period are negotiable at this stage. Getting a smaller holdback or a shorter survival period into the LOI gives your attorney a position to defend when the Purchase Agreement is drafted. Trying to negotiate the holdback for the first time in the Purchase Agreement—after you're already in exclusivity—is a much harder conversation.

The purchase price allocation framework: Not every LOI addresses this, but if yours does, the allocation between goodwill and other asset categories has real tax consequences for you. Getting favorable language in the LOI anchors the negotiation when the Purchase Agreement is drafted. Your CPA should review any allocation language before you sign.

None of this requires being adversarial. The LOI negotiation is professional and expected—every serious buyer knows that sellers have attorneys and that the LOI will be marked up. What it requires is knowing what matters before you're in the room, so you don't give up ground you didn't know you had.

17

DUE DILIGENCE: EXPECT IT, PREP FOR IT, OWN IT

Once the LOI is signed and the deal is moving toward closing, you enter the scariest phase of the whole process: due diligence.

Due diligence is the period during which the buyer—with the help of accountants, attorneys, and sometimes industry consultants—digs into every corner of your business to verify that what you've represented is true. Tax returns, P&Ls, bank statements, leases, employment agreements, insurance policies, payroll records, vendor contracts, customer agreements. Everything.

It's invasive. It's exhausting. And it almost always surfaces something unexpected.

WHAT THEY'RE REALLY LOOKING FOR

Buyers and their advisors are not trying to find a reason to reduce the price—at least, ideal buyers aren't. They're trying to verify that the story they've been told is true, and to understand the real risk profile of what they're acquiring.

The primary concern is financial accuracy. Do the numbers match? Can the reported earnings be verified? Are there patterns in the bank statements that contradict what the financials show? The buyers who've been burned in previous deals—and many experienced buyers have been—become forensic accountants when they do due diligence. They're not paranoid; they're careful.

Beyond finances, they're looking at operational risk. Is the business compliant with relevant employment laws? Are all contractors properly classified? Are there unresolved legal issues? Is the lease clean and transferable? Are there any long-term commitments or liabilities that weren't disclosed?

SOMETHING WILL COME UP—HERE'S WHAT TO DO

I have worked on more than seventy transactions. I can count on one hand the number that made it through due diligence without a single surprise emerging. This is normal. It's expected. It is not a deal killer on its own. What matters is how you handle it.

The sellers who get through due diligence successfully are the ones who are proactive and transparent. When something comes up, they acknowledge it quickly, explain the context accurately, and come to the table with a proposed solution—whether that's a correction, a price adjustment, an escrow holdback, a warranty, or another mechanism that gives the buyer confidence.

The sellers who lose deals during due diligence are the ones who get defensive, minimize legitimate concerns, appear to be hiding things, or respond to every question with frustration. Remember: the buyer is about to hand you a significant sum of money. They are entitled to look carefully at what they're buying. The goal here is to be reassuring.

FIND AND DISCLOSE YOUR SKELETONS UP FRONT

The best preparation for due diligence is to do your own version first. Walk through your business the way a skeptical buyer would. Pull every agreement and review it. Review your financials for anything unexplained. Have your CPA or a quality-of-earnings firm conduct a formal analysis. Check your HR compliance. Review your lease assignment provisions.

Find the problems yourself, fix what can be fixed, and be prepared to explain what can't. A seller who enters due diligence already knowing where the skeletons are—and who has a story ready for each one—is in a completely different place than one who gets blindsided alongside the buyer. This is exactly why the quality of earnings review from Chapter Five and the HR audit from Chapter Eight matter so much. They find the skeletons before a buyer does.

Build a due diligence data room early in the process—a digital folder containing all the key documents a buyer will request. Having this organized and ready communicates professionalism and confidence, and compresses the timeline. The seller who walks into due diligence with everything organized and nothing to hide controls the process. That seller is you. (Use Appendix A's checklist to know exactly what to include.)

18

WHEN A DEAL FALLS APART

Sometimes deals fall apart. Not because anyone did anything wrong. Not because your business wasn't worth selling. A deal can die because the buyer's SBA financing falls through at the last moment. Because something surfaces in due diligence that neither party anticipated. Because the buyer gets cold feet three weeks before closing. Because life intervenes on their side in ways that have nothing to do with you.

It happens. It has happened to clients of mine who prepared thoroughly, priced correctly, and did everything right. And when it does, the experience is genuinely brutal—months of emotional investment, the process of telling your key people, the anticipation of what comes next— all of it collapses in a conversation that usually takes about fifteen minutes.

This is what I tell sellers when it happens.

First: Hopefully, you still have backup offers on standby. But if you don't, it's worth pausing. The instinct is to move fast—to get another deal going before the anxiety of the failed one settles in. Resist that instinct. Give yourself two to four weeks before doing anything. Use that time to debrief honestly on what happened. Did due diligence surface a real problem you need to fix? Was the pricing wrong? Was it genuinely bad luck with that specific buyer? The answer shapes your next move.

Second: Carefully manage what your staff and community know. If your team found out about the sale—which may have been unavoidable by that stage—you need to address it directly rather than go quiet. Something simple and honest works: "We were in a process that didn't come together. The business is strong, and I'm not going anywhere right now." That's true, it's reassuring, and it doesn't require more detail than you want to give.

Third: Understand what the failed process revealed about your business and your buyer pool. If you had strong interest but the deal died in financing, you may need to reduce the price or position toward cash buyers or PE. If it died because something came up in due diligence, you have a specific problem to fix before re-listing. If the buyer simply walked, ask your broker for a frank assessment of whether the asking price and the market reality are aligned.

Fourth: A failed transaction does not reduce the value of your studio. It reduces your energy and your confidence, which is why timing your re-entry matters. Almost every seller I know who went through a failed deal, took the time to regroup, and came back to market prepared—sold. Often for more than the original deal would have paid.

WHEN THE BUYER COMES BACK WITH A LOWER NUMBER

Almost every transaction has a moment that nobody fully prepares sellers for, and it lands harder than anything else in the process: due diligence surfaces an issue or a concern, and the buyer comes back with a revised offer. A lower price. A larger holdback. A new condition. After months of relationship-building, after signing the LOI with excitement on both sides, after believing you were headed to closing, the number changes.

This is not a betrayal. It is, statistically, the most normal thing that happens in a deal. The question isn't whether to expect it. The question is how to evaluate it and what to do about it.

First: Separate legitimate findings from opportunistic ones. A legitimate renegotiation is anchored in a specific deal point discovered in due diligence—workers who were misclassified with real back-tax liability attached, a lease issue that was disclosed but more complex than represented, or financials that don't reconcile in a material way. The buyer has found a real risk and is asking you to share it. That is a reasonable conversation.

An opportunistic renegotiation looks different: the finding is vague, the price reduction is disproportionate to the actual issue, and the timing comes suspiciously late in the process when you're most emotionally invested. Buyers who planned to renegotiate all along use due diligence as the vehicle.

Most buyers who come back with a lower number have found something genuine—approach the conversation that way first. The rare buyer who planned to renegotiate all along will reveal themselves through the pattern: multiple vague findings, a lump-sum reduction unconnected to any specific issue, escalating pressure as closing approaches. Your broker will recognize it. Learn to trust that read.

Second: Involve your broker before you respond to anything. The instinct when a buyer comes back with a lower number is to react—to feel hurt, to get defensive, to either concede immediately or dig in emotionally. Neither serves you. Your broker has seen this before. They can evaluate whether the finding justifies the ask, suggest counter-structures that address the buyer's concern without simply reducing your price, and manage the temperature of the conversation before it becomes adversarial.

Third: Understand your alternatives before you negotiate. Your position in a post-diligence renegotiation depends entirely on whether you have other buyers who could step in. If you went to market with multiple offers and your second-best buyer is still warm, you negotiate from a fundamentally different position than if this is your only path. This is one more reason competition at the LOI stage matters so much

—it doesn't just affect the initial price, it affects your ability to hold firm when pressure arrives later.

Fourth: Know your walk-away point before the conversation starts. What is the minimum outcome that still makes this deal worth doing? What would you do if this buyer walked entirely? Having clear answers to those questions—privately, before you sit across the table—prevents you from making decisions in the heat of the moment that you'd make differently with a clearer head.

The post-diligence renegotiation is where deals are won or lost. Sellers who are prepared for it—who can evaluate findings objectively and negotiate from a grounded position—close. Sellers who are blind-sided by it, or who have no alternative and no floor, give away more than they had to.

19

HOW YOUR BUYER WILL PAY FOR YOUR BUSINESS

You've probably never thought much about how your buyer will come up with the money. Most sellers haven't. But understanding it will change how you think about your financials, your pricing, and your buyer pool.

The SBA 7(a) loan program is the primary way boutique fitness businesses in the $250,000 to $5 million range get acquired. Understanding how it works explains why certain things are required from your financials—and why certain deal structures are possible, and others aren't.

HOW THE LOAN ACTUALLY WORKS

The SBA does not lend money directly. Instead, it guarantees a portion of loans made by approved lenders—banks and credit unions that participate in the SBA program. Because the government guarantees repayment if the borrower defaults, lenders are willing to finance business acquisitions they would not otherwise finance.

The buyer typically puts down 10 percent of the purchase price and finances the rest through an SBA loan. The loan is repaid over ten years at interest rates tied to the prime rate. Monthly payments come out of the business's cash flow.

WHY YOUR BOOKS DETERMINE THE LOAN

For the business to qualify for SBA financing, the lender needs to see that your SDE comfortably covers the annual loan payment—typically by at least 25 percent (a ratio called DSCR; see Appendix B). If the math doesn't work, the buyer can't get the loan, and the deal doesn't happen. The same business with three years of clean financials versus three years of artificially suppressed profit is the difference between a closeable deal and one that dies in underwriting. This is the direct consequence of the tax strategy tradeoff covered in Chapter Five.

THE SELLER NOTE AND WHAT IT MEANS

In some SBA transactions, sellers are required to carry a small amount of seller financing—typically up to 10 percent of the purchase price—to demonstrate confidence in the business. I know that's not what most sellers want to hear. Here's why it's more manageable than it sounds: the seller note is typically a small portion of a much larger transaction, and it signals to the bank that you believe in what you're selling.

The note has specific rules under SBA guidelines—including that it's typically required to be on full standby, meaning no payments to you at all for the duration of the SBA loan. On a ten-year loan, that means you may wait a decade to collect on that portion. This often comes as a surprise to sellers. SBA guidelines also govern earnouts, stock sales, and goodwill allocations—all of which affect your deal structure. Work with a broker and attorney experienced in SBA-financed transactions before you receive your first offer. The rules are specific, and violations can jeopardize the financing.

EARNOUTS: WHEN THEY MAKE SENSE AND WHEN THEY DON'T

An earnout is when part of the purchase price depends on the business hitting defined targets after you've sold it—revenue, membership, EBITDA. Sounds clean on paper: the seller gets paid if performance holds, and the buyer gets protection if it doesn't. In reality, earnouts are far riskier for sellers than they appear.

Here's why: once you've sold, you don't control whether those targets get hit. The new owner does. They decide on pricing, staffing, class schedule, and marketing spend. If they make moves that tank revenue—bad decisions or just different priorities—your earnout shrinks. You have zero operational control but all the financial risk. This is why I push sellers hard against earnouts, especially big ones.

That said, they can make sense in specific spots. If you had one anomalously strong year that inflated your numbers, an earnout can bridge the valuation gap fairly. If you're staying involved post-close and actually contributing to results, an earnout tied to that work makes sense. And sometimes an earnout is the only way a deal closes at all.

I had a client—a high-end Pilates studio doing $800,000 in revenue —sell to an incoming instructor who wanted to buy in but didn't want to pay full price because the owner was the draw. They structured an earnout: $400,000 at close, with an additional $200,000 if membership stayed above 250 for year one. The seller stayed on part-time to help with the transition. Revenue stayed flat. Membership held at 260. She got the full earnout. But that was because the new owner was competent and they aligned on what "success" looked like. I've seen the opposite just as often—buyer makes different choices, revenue slides, and the seller gets nothing because the targets were realistic when set but never hit.

If you do agree to an earnout, negotiate hard on three things:

- Make it short—one year maximum.
- Use objective, unmovable metrics like total revenue instead of EBITDA (which buyers can manipulate).

- Get clear dispute resolution in writing that doesn't require litigation. Get your M&A attorney to draft this carefully. A bad earn out is uncollectable even when the business performs. Have your CPA and attorney review the earnout terms together before you sign.

The cleanest deals have no earnouts. If your books are clean and your numbers check out, a buyer demanding a large earnout is either undercapitalized or doesn't believe what you've told them. Both are worth a hard look before you agree.

HOW BUYERS BREAK THE CEILING

As covered in Chapter Four, SBA lenders are generally comfortable financing deals up to approximately 3x to 3.5x SDE. Above that, you need cash buyers or private equity at the table—which is one more reason a broad buyer pool matters.

WHAT YOU'LL ACTUALLY NET

The purchase price is not the money that hits your bank account. There's a real distance between the two.

I had a client, "Maya," sell her studio for $1.1 million. Eight years, solid unit economics, good team. On paper, it was a $1.1 million transaction. Here's what actually happened.

Broker commission at 10 percent was $110,000. Her CPA and M&A attorney combined ran about $35,000. That left $955,000.

Then the tax piece. The range is typically thirty to forty cents on the dollar. Some states are worse than others. That left roughly $650,000.

The purchase agreement allocated the $1.1 million across the following buckets: goodwill (taxed as long-term capital gains), depreciation recapture on equipment (taxed as ordinary income), and a noncompete (taxed as ordinary income). The way deals are typically structured, buyers push hard to load more value into equipment bucket because they get faster tax deductions. Sellers should push back.

Maya's deal was allocated roughly $700,000 to goodwill, $300,000 to equipment, and $100,000 to the non-compete.

One variable: if you take a seller note, installment sale treatment spreads your gain recognition across years instead of concentrating it all in year one, which can lower your total tax bill. Model both scenarios with your CPA—all-cash versus seller note—before you commit to one.

Get a CPA who's done business transactions, not just annual returns. Understand your net number before you set your asking price.

20

WHAT YOU'RE SIGNING

A few years back, I brokered a deal for a 3,500-square-foot Pilates studio in the Midwest. Clean business, solid numbers, owner had run it for eight years. The buyer was a regional chain looking to expand. Everything moved smoothly. Seller got her wire transfer, celebrated, and moved on to her next thing.

Fourteen months post-closing—so we're still in the holdback window—the buyer's accountant finds something. The studio had misclassified a part-time front-desk person for the entire time the seller owned it. Should've been a W-2, was a 1099. Back payroll taxes, employment taxes, penalties. The buyer made a claim against the holdback for about $28,000.

The seller called me in a fury. She insisted the person had always wanted to be independent. Maybe true, maybe not—didn't matter. What mattered was what was in writing, and what she'd signed in the Purchase Agreement. The buyer had documentation. The holdback was there exactly for this moment.

Here's the thing: if that seller had come to the closing table with clean HR records and a seller-commissioned QoE (see Chapter Five), that claim would have been much harder for the buyer to sustain.

That's what reps and warranties, and the holdback backing them up, actually mean in a real deal.

REPS AND WARRANTIES: MAKING PROMISES IN WRITING

When you sign the Purchase Agreement, you're not just signing a sales document. You're signing a set of formal legal statements about your business. You're representing that your financials are accurate. That there are no undisclosed liabilities. That employees are properly classified. That there are no pending lawsuits or regulatory violations. That everything you've told the buyer is true and complete.

These representations and warranties don't expire the moment the deal closes. If any of them turn out to be wrong—even if you made the mistake honestly—the buyer can come back to you for money. That's where the holdback comes in.

A holdback is part of your purchase price that doesn't hit your bank account at closing. It's often 5 to 10 percent. It sits in an escrow account, typically held for twelve to eighteen months, as insurance against the buyer finding problems post-closing. If they discover that a misclassified employee, six months in, owes back taxes because of it, they make a claim against the holdback. You're not just signing paperwork—you're signing away access to that money until the buyer is comfortable nothing's going to surface.

Three things matter here. The holdback is negotiable. If your books are clean, your HR is documented, and you commissioned a QoE before going to market, you're in a strong position to push for no holdback at all, or at least a smaller one with a shorter period. This is why the preparation work throughout this book matters. You walk into a closing with three years of clean, organized financials and proper employee files, and suddenly, you're not the seller who looks like they're hiding something.

The language matters enormously. Vague language in the Purchase Agreement favors the buyer. Specific thresholds, defined materiality standards, and clear definitions of what counts as a breach—that favors you. Your attorney needs to read this carefully and push back on vague language.

Representations and warranties insurance exists. For larger transactions, it's increasingly standard. It allows you to shrink the holdback or eliminate it entirely by shifting the post-closing risk to an insurance company rather than keeping it in escrow. It's worth exploring with your attorney.

Closing day is not the finish line for your legal exposure. Get an attorney who negotiates holdback terms on your behalf, rather than rubber-stamping what the buyer's lawyer sends over.

PERSONAL LIABILITY: YOU'RE SIGNING THIS, NOT YOUR BUSINESS

Here's something most sellers don't grasp until they're at the closing table, and by then it's a late conversation to be having. When you sell a boutique fitness studio in an asset sale, the buyer has little faith in suing the LLC after the deal closes. In most cases, the LLC gets dissolved or wound down in the months following closing. The entity that made all those representations and warranties ceases to exist. So if the buyer has a legitimate claim six months later, they need someone real to pursue.

That someone is you.

Buyers almost always require sellers to sign the reps and warranties in their personal capacity, not just as the business entity. It's called "personal indemnification" or "personal liability on the reps"—the terminology varies. What it means is that your personal assets could be on the line if something goes wrong post-closing, not just the business assets.

This is standard. Every experienced seller's attorney will tell you it's how asset sales work, and pushing back entirely won't get you anywhere. What *is* worth negotiating is the scope and duration.

Here's what that looks like in practice: on a typical boutique fitness deal, your total personal exposure to general representations usually falls between 10 and 20 percent of the purchase price. On a $1,000,000 deal, that's roughly $100,000 to $200,000. The window the buyer has to bring a claim—the survival period—is typically twelve to twenty-four months. After that, they can't come after you anymore. There's also a minimum threshold, called a basket, before the buyer can make any claim at all—usually around 1 percent of the purchase price. Your attorney should be fighting for all three protections: a cap, a short survival period, and a basket. (See Appendix B for full definitions of these terms.)

Personal liability on your reps is coming, no matter how you've structured your business. The best protection isn't trying to dodge it— it's making sure your representations are accurate, your disclosures are complete, and your attorney has negotiated terms that limit your exposure to what's reasonable and time-bound.

THE NON-COMPETE: TAKE IT SERIOUSLY

Your Purchase Agreement will include a non-compete clause. You agree not to open or work for a competing studio within a defined radius for a defined period—typically two to five years. Some buyers push for longer. Enforceability varies wildly by state. Have your attorney review the specific terms and geography before you sign. Different states treat this differently, and you need to know what you're actually agreeing to.

But beyond the legal piece, think about what the non-compete represents. You sold your team and your clients, and you're promising not to poach them after the sale. Honor that.

THE CLOSING STATEMENT: WHAT ACTUALLY HITS YOUR ACCOUNT

Even after you understand the tax picture, there's one more layer between your purchase price and the wire that arrives in your bank account: the closing statement. This is a line-by-line reconciliation of every dollar that flows at closing, and first-time sellers are regularly surprised by how different the final number looks from the headline price. Here's what typically shows up on a boutique fitness closing statement.

Model your net proceeds from the purchase price down, not up, from what you hope to keep. Start with the purchase price, subtract the broker commission, subtract the estimated tax liability, subtract the outstanding package balance, subtract the holdback, and adjust for rent and deposit prorations. The number you're left with is closer to what you'll actually receive at closing. Your attorney and broker should walk you through a projected closing statement before you sign the closing paperwork to avoid any surprises on the day of closing.

SETTING THE NEW OWNER UP TO SUCCEED

In almost every transaction, there's a transition period—a defined time after closing during which you remain available to help the new owner get oriented. This is typically two to four weeks of intensive support followed by some period of availability for questions, often thirty to sixty days.

The transition period matters more than most sellers realize—especially the ones who are emotionally ready to be done. The new owner needs to meet key staff members, understand the software systems, be carefully introduced to the member community, get their hands on all vendor relationships, and understand every idiosyncrasy of the business that isn't in any manual.

Go into the transition period with generosity. Your job is to set this person up to succeed. The community you built, the staff you hired, the members who trust you—their well-being now depends on this transition going well. Give the new owner the best possible start, not because you're contractually obligated to, but because it's the right thing to do.

THE PRACTICAL REALITY OF TRANSITION

Two to four weeks sounds short. In practice, it's a very compressed window to transfer everything a new owner needs to know to run your business. The sellers who do it well treat the transition period as a project with a defined scope and a checklist—not a vague period of being available.

Week one is the most intensive—you're physically present, introducing the new owner to staff, walking them through systems, and making key vendor calls together. By weeks two through four, your role shifts from leading to advising as the new owner starts making decisions on their own. After the intensive period, stay available for thirty to sixty days as a safety net. When the new owner texts you at 7 am because an instructor called in sick and they don't know the backup protocol, respond. The goodwill matters for the community you're leaving behind.

One practical note: your general liability and workers' compensation policies run on a policy year, not aligned to your closing date. Coordinate with your insurance broker to ensure there's no gap in coverage at the moment of transfer. The Purchase Agreement should specify who is responsible for coverage through the closing date, and the new owner's insurance should be confirmed before the keys change hands.

THE DAY IT'S REALLY REAL

The mechanics of closing depend on the deal structure, but in a typical SBA-financed transaction, here's what happens. Your attorney and the buyer's attorney have spent the preceding weeks drafting and negotiating the Purchase Agreement, the Bill of Sale, and any related documents. They've also worked with the landlords and their attorneys to finalize the lease assignments. The buyer's bank has completed its underwriting. Everyone has reviewed and agreed to the final forms.

On closing day, signatures happen—typically in sequence, most often electronically, increasingly via digital signing platforms. Once everything is executed, the bank wires funds to an escrow account or directly to you. When the funds are confirmed, the keys change hands. Your team of broker and attorney should coordinate the flow of this process, ensuring no document is missing and no step is skipped.

The transition period is the last chapter of your ownership. Do it the way you did everything else—with care.

21

THE DAY YOU STOP
BEING THE OWNER

Closing day. After years of preparation, marketing, negotiation, and due diligence, the day finally arrives. Documents will be signed. Wire transfers will be confirmed. And then, somewhere in the middle of all the paperwork, a moment will hit that's hard to describe unless you've been through it: you will no longer be the owner.

It is at once the most anticlimactic and the most profound experience of this entire journey.

WHAT TO SAY WHEN YOU TELL YOUR STAFF

The most emotionally charged conversation in any sale is telling the staff. My general guidance: tell key team members once the deal is materially close—meaning the Purchase Agreement is signed, the Lease Assignment is approved, and the deal is set to close. You want to be well past the point of no return before you have this conversation.

When you do have the conversation, be honest, warm, and forward-looking. Share why you made this decision. Affirm the value of each person's contribution. Introduce the new owner with genuine enthusiasm. Acknowledge that change is hard. Give people space to feel whatever they feel—some will be excited, some anxious, some sad. All of those responses are understandable and valid. They'll quickly start thinking about what this means for them. That's natural.

WHAT TO SAY WHEN YOU TELL YOUR COMMUNITY

Member communication is similarly delicate and similarly important. Most successful transitions involve a warm, personal message from the outgoing owner—via email, sometimes via video—introducing the new owner and framing the transition positively. The tone should be celebratory. You're not leaving because something is wrong. You're passing this community to someone who shares your values and is ready to take it forward.

The greatest risk in a transition is membership attrition. If members feel like the community they loved is ending, they'll cancel. The goal of your communication and the new owner's early actions is to reassure them that what made this place special is continuing—and that good things are ahead.

THE FIRST MONDAY WITH NOWHERE TO BE

Something happens after closing that nobody fully prepares you for, and I've watched it surprise seller after seller—including myself when I went through it.

You've been "the owner" for however many years. That title is not just a business description—it's part of who you are. It's how people introduce you at parties. It's the answer to "What do you do?" at every social gathering. It's woven into your friendships, your daily routine, your sense of purpose. When you walk into a room full of people in your industry, your identity is clear and known. You belong somewhere specific.

When you sell, all of that changes in a day. Sometimes you're ready for that change—you've been dreaming about it, building toward it, and when the moment comes, you feel freer than you've felt in years.

But sometimes—and this catches sellers by surprise—you feel lost. Not sad exactly, and not regretful, but unmoored in a way that's hard to explain to people who haven't experienced it. The calendar has no obligations. The phone doesn't ring with problems to solve. The staff isn't texting. And instead of relief, there's a strange hollowness.

I've had sellers call me in the weeks after closing in a state I can only describe as mourning. The money is in the bank. The papers are signed. By every external measure, it was a success. And they're devastated. Not because they regret selling. But because something is gone that they didn't know how much they needed—not the work itself, but the identity that came with it. The certainty of knowing exactly who you are and what you're supposed to be doing today.

One client—a studio owner who sold after twelve years—told me that the hardest moment wasn't signing the papers or saying goodbye to the staff. It was the first Monday morning after closing, when she woke up at 6:30 out of habit and realized there was nowhere she was required to be. "I sat at my kitchen table for an hour," she told me, "and I couldn't decide if I was the freest I'd ever been or the most lost." Both, I told her. You're allowed to be both.

I take these calls seriously. Because this is part of the process—and it matters. Naming it in advance, knowing the disorientation is coming and is normal, makes it easier to move through.

THE LOVE BEHIND THE GUILT

Many sellers carry a guilt that's hard to name. It sounds something like: "Who am I to walk away from something so many people depend on?" This guilt is real, and it comes from a good place—from genuine care about the people you've built a community with. I don't want to dismiss it. But I do want to offer a different frame.

Selling your business responsibly—finding a buyer committed to continuing it, who will take care of your staff, who will honor the culture you built—is stewardship, not abandonment. You are not deserting your people. You are ensuring the business has the leadership, the resources, and the fresh energy it needs to continue. In many cases, a new owner will do things you never had the time or capital to do: renovate the space, expand the schedule, add modalities, and hire the instructor you always wanted but couldn't afford.

The real abandonment—the version I've seen lead to genuine regret—is running a business past the point where you have energy for it. Showing up every day with less than your best. Watching membership slowly erode because the culture started to shift when you started to check out, and you didn't leave because you felt too responsible. The intentional exit is not abandonment. It's the most loving thing you can do for what you built.

THE PEACE IS COMING

The emotional arc of selling a business is remarkably consistent: relief when the decision is made, anxiety through the process, exhaustion in the final push to closing, and then a complicated aftermath of euphoria and grief arriving simultaneously. And then—almost universally—peace.

EPILOGUE: WHAT COMES NEXT

From where I'm sitting, I can see the sparkling reflection of the Mediterranean. My kids are somewhere nearby, navigating the streets and speaking a new language with an ease that would have seemed impossible a year ago.

Sunshine, lounge chair, palm trees. It's a perfect cliché. None of this happened by accident.

The life I'm living right now is the direct result of dreams Karson and I made together more than a decade ago, when we walked into a little yoga studio in our neighborhood and decided to bet on ourselves.

I want to say something specific about Karson here, because this book is dedicated to her and she deserves more than a dedication page.

Our yoga studio was what it was because of her. Not because of the systems I built or the operational discipline I brought from the hotel world—those mattered, but they were not the reason our community showed up. They showed up because of her.

Her classes merged yoga and positive psychology like a TED Talk for your soul. She remembered everyone's names and their injuries. She held space for all of us to work through whatever we needed to. She taught us about manifestation and the Law of Attraction. I used to be a little cynical, but she has proven that it is real.

What this work has given me professionally, she has made possible personally. What our family gets to do now—living in Spain, watching our kids find their way in a world bigger than either of us grew up in—is downstream of the choice we made together when we bought that studio, and the choice we made again when we sold it right. And every choice we've made ever since to follow our dreams.

You too can manifest your dream exit. Oftentimes, the hardest question is "What do you want?" If you can describe it in great detail and believe it's realistic and possible, you're already halfway there.

— Mitch McGinley
    Sitges, Spain
    May 2026

APPENDIX A: THE EXIT READINESS CHECKLIST

Use this checklist to assess where you are in your exit preparation. A "yes" on most of these items suggests you're in a strong position to sell. A "no" on any of them is a signal to get to work. You'll see this checklist referenced throughout the book—those references point here.

FINANCIAL READINESS

- ☐ Three years of clean, professionally prepared federal tax returns showing real profitability
- ☐ Monthly profit-and-loss statements for the trailing twenty-four months
- ☐ Bank statements that align with your P&L and tax returns
- ☐ A clear list of all owner addbacks with documentation
- ☐ No significant unexplained variances between financial periods
- ☐ A quality of earnings analysis completed or at least planned

OPERATIONAL READINESS

- ☐ A general manager or operations lead who runs the day-to-day without you
- ☐ Documented operational procedures for all key processes
- ☐ An instructor roster deep enough to survive the loss of one or two key staff members
- ☐ Technology systems that are current and documented
- ☐ The business can operate for two weeks without you present (the vacation test)

LEGAL AND COMPLIANCE READINESS

- ☐ All employees and contractors properly classified under current law
- ☐ PTO, sick leave, and benefits policies documented and compliant with applicable state law
- ☐ Workers' compensation and liability insurance current and appropriate
- ☐ Employment agreements in place with key staff
- ☐ No unresolved legal disputes or regulatory violations

LEASE READINESS

- ☐ A lease with at least three years remaining (ideally five-plus)
- ☐ Assignment provisions that allow transfer to a new owner without landlord veto
- ☐ A landlord relationship that is cooperative, not adversarial
- ☐ Personal guarantees understood and a plan to negotiate release at sale

MARKETING AND MEMBER READINESS

- ☐ Stable or growing active membership over the trailing twelve months
- ☐ Membership contracts that transfer with the business
- ☐ A clear understanding of member demographics, tenure, and retention rates
- ☐ A business reputation that reflects well on the brand
- ☐ Outstanding gift card and prepaid package balances documented, with a proposed treatment agreed upon for closing

DUE DILIGENCE DATA ROOM

- ☐ Three years of tax returns organized and accessible
- ☐ Monthly P&Ls and bank statements for the trailing two years
- ☐ The lease and all amendments
- ☐ All employment agreements and contractor agreements
- ☐ Insurance certificates
- ☐ Software and vendor agreements
- ☐ Any other material contracts

Net Proceeds Worksheet

Use this worksheet to calculate your net proceeds from the sale:

Sale Price: $__________
  Subtract:

- Broker commission: ~10%
- Attorney: ~$10,000+
- Accounting/CPA: ~$2,500+
- Other professional fees (QoE, investment advisor): ~$20,000+, (if necessary)
- Tax Estimate from CPA: ~30-40% of tax basis
- Holdback or escrow amount: ~10%
- Any loan payoffs such as SBA or equipment

Net Proceeds: $__________

Work with your CPA to model these based on your purchase price and actual allocation. How the purchase price is allocated between equipment, goodwill, and non-compete affects your tax bill significantly.

APPENDIX B: KEY TERMS
EVERY SELLER SHOULD KNOW

The business transaction world has its own vocabulary. These are the terms that come up most often in boutique fitness sales. References to this glossary appear throughout the book wherever these terms are introduced.

VALUATION TERMS

Seller's Discretionary Earnings (SDE): The real cash your business generates for its owner, after adjusting for owner compensation, non-recurring expenses, and personal items. The number buyers and lenders use to value your business. See Chapters 3 and 5.

EBITDA: Earnings before interest, taxes, depreciation, and amortization. More commonly used in larger transactions and private equity deals.

Multiple: The number by which SDE is multiplied to arrive at a valuation—e.g., 3x on $200,000 SDE equals $600,000. See Chapter 4.

Quality of Earnings (QoE): An independent accounting analysis that verifies your financials. Increasingly commissioned by sellers before going to market. See Chapter 5.

Addback: An expense added back to net income because a new owner would not incur it—owner salary above market rate, personal vehicle expenses, health insurance, one-time events. See Chapter 5.

DEAL TERMS

Letter of Intent (LOI): A non-binding document outlining key terms of a proposed transaction. Initiates exclusive due diligence. See Chapter 16.

Purchase Agreement (PA): The binding legal contract documenting final sale terms. Sometimes called a Purchase and Sale Agreement or Asset Purchase Agreement. See Chapter 20.

Asset Sale vs. Stock Sale: In an asset sale, the buyer purchases specific assets but not the legal entity. In a stock sale, the buyer purchases the entity, inheriting all assets and liabilities. Most small business transactions are asset sales.

Earnout: A portion of the purchase price paid after closing based on defined performance targets. Carries risk for sellers. See Chapter 19.

Seller Note: Part of the purchase price structured as a loan from the buyer, paid over time. See Chapter 19.

Indemnification Cap: The maximum dollar amount the seller can be held liable for under representations and warranties after closing. General cap typically runs 10 to 20 percent of the purchase price.

Indemnification Basket: A minimum threshold of losses before the buyer can make an indemnification claim. Market standard is roughly 0.5 percent to 1 percent of the purchase price.

Personal Indemnification Obligation: The requirement that the seller sign reps and warranties in their individual capacity, not just as the business entity. Standard in asset sales. Scope and duration are negotiable.

SBA 7(a) Loan: A government-guaranteed loan commonly used by buyers to finance acquisitions with as little as 10 percent down. See Chapter 19.

Due Diligence: The period during which the buyer investigates all aspects of the business. Typically thirty to ninety days. See Chapter 17.

Escrow Holdback: An amount withheld from the seller's proceeds at closing and held until specified conditions are met. See Chapter 20.

Non-Compete Agreement: A provision restricting the seller from competing within a defined geography and time period.

Debt Service Coverage Ratio (DSCR): The ratio of annual SDE to annual loan payment. SBA lenders typically require at least 1.25.

APPENDIX C: IF YOU OWN YOUR BUILDING

Most of this book assumes you lease your space—most boutique fitness owners do. But if you own the real property, you have a different set of options that deserve direct attention.

The first option is to sell the real estate with the business as a combined package. This simplifies the transaction and appeals to buyers who want to own both. It makes a lot of sense for businesses with unique buildouts. The valuation becomes more complex—you're selling two assets, each valued differently—and the buyer pool narrows to those willing to acquire both. SBA financing can cover both, and in some scenarios, this opens up creative financing and tax strategies.

The second option is to sell the business but keep the building. You become the landlord. The buyer gets the business and a landlord who should be incredibly accommodating. You get ongoing rental income and preserve your connection to the community without the operational headaches. This structure can sometimes produce a better combined outcome than selling both together, because it separates two assets that different buyer pools may value differently. It also gives you a presumably appreciating asset. One risk worth weighing: your rental income depends entirely on the new owner's success. If the business struggles, you hold a commercial space with concentrated tenant risk and potentially no income. Understand that exposure before choosing this path.

The third option—selling the building but keeping the business—is rare, but if you can sell the building at a strong price and lock in favorable lease terms, it's worth considering.

Each structure has different tax treatment and different buyer implications. This is not a decision to make alone—it requires your CPA, a real estate attorney, and possibly an advisor who specializes in sale-leaseback structures. If you own your space, bring this question to your team early. The right structure dictates how you approach everything else.

APPENDIX D: FRANCHISE AND MULTI-LOCATION VARIABLES

If you own more than one location, you face a decision that single-location owners don't: do you go to market with all locations as a single package, or do you sell them individually?

The case for packaging: a multi-unit portfolio commands a higher multiple than individual locations sold separately. Buyers—especially PE and serial operators—pay a premium for scale and proven replicability. A two-location business generating $400,000 in combined SDE will typically sell at a higher multiple than two separate $200,000-SDE businesses would. If your systems are strong and your locations are performing, packaging is almost always the better financial outcome. And one transaction instead of two makes the whole exit simpler.

The case for selling separately: if one location is performing significantly better than another, packaging them forces you to defend the weaker one throughout the entire process. A struggling location can drag down the multiple on the whole portfolio. In that scenario, selling the strong location first—at a premium—and then dealing with the weaker one separately may yield a better combined result, even if the total price is lower on paper.

There's also the buyer pool. The buyer who can acquire a two-location package is a different person from the buyer who can acquire one.

Multi-location deals typically require larger SBA loans, more capital, or PE involvement—which narrows the pool. A single-location deal can attract a much wider range of qualified buyers, leading to more competition and better terms.

My general guidance: if both locations are healthy and your systems are replicable, package them. If there's a material performance gap between locations, talk to your broker honestly about whether you're better served by a portfolio sale or a sequential strategy. There's no universal answer. But knowing which question you're asking—portfolio premium or buyer pool breadth—lets you have a better conversation with your broker from day one.

Specialty formats like IV drip bars, cryotherapy studios, or medically adjacent wellness businesses have smaller buyer pools and can command premium multiples if positioned correctly—but finding the right buyer requires a more targeted approach.

IF YOU'RE A FRANCHISEE: WHAT'S DIFFERENT

If you own a franchise location—Club Pilates, F45, Orangetheory, barre3, Rumble, or any of the dozens of other brands—the five elements still apply. But you face a layer of complexity that independent owners don't, and if you're not prepared for it, it will slow your transaction, cost you money, or both.

Start with your franchisor's right of first refusal. Most franchise agreements give the franchisor the right to step in and purchase your business at the same price and terms you've negotiated with an outside buyer. This means that after months of finding the right buyer, negotiating a price, and reaching an agreement, your franchisor can take their place. This right exists to protect brand standards and ensure the franchisor controls who carries their name—a legitimate interest that benefits every franchisee in the system. In practice, most franchisors don't exercise it. But the possibility shapes the entire transaction. Most franchise agreements include explicit disclosure obligations around a pending sale, and attempting to conceal one is generally inadvisable regardless of what your specific agreement says. The relationship you've maintained with your franchise development contact matters here.

Then there's the transfer fee. Most franchise agreements require the buyer or seller to pay a transfer fee to the franchisor at closing—typically somewhere between $10,000 and $25,000 per location, depending on the brand. Transfer fee structures vary significantly by franchisor and can change; confirm the current terms in your franchise disclosure document and agreement, not from secondhand sources. This fee may come out of your proceeds and should be accounted for in your net proceeds calculation from day one, not discovered at closing.

Your franchisor also has the right to approve or reject the incoming buyer. They're looking for someone who meets their financial qualifications, passes their background check, and can complete their training program. A buyer who is perfect for your business may not be the buyer your franchisor wants. Those criteria exist to protect the brand and every other franchisee in the system, which ultimately protects the value of your location, too. I've seen deals fall apart at the finish line because the franchisor declined to approve the buyer. Knowing your brand's approval criteria before you start marketing the business saves enormous frustration.

Most franchise systems also require the incoming owner to complete the brand's full training program before or shortly after closing. That program takes time—sometimes weeks—and it affects your transition timeline. Build it into your planning.

Finally, understand how franchise royalties and fees affect your SDE. Any looming increase in monthly royalties, the marketing fund contribution, and any technology fees are real ongoing expenses that reduce the earnings a buyer acquires. Make sure your SDE calculation reflects these accurately, and be prepared to explain them clearly to buyers who may not be familiar with the franchise model.

The bottom line: franchisees can absolutely sell—and often command strong prices because brand recognition and built-in systems give buyers confidence. But the path runs through your franchisor, and the sooner you understand what your franchise agreement requires, the better positioned you'll be.

APPENDIX E: RESOURCES AND NEXT STEPS

Congratulations—you've made it to the end of this book. Here's how to take what you've learned and turn it into action.

FREE RESOURCES AT BOUTIQUE FITNESS BROKER

Everything you need to start your exit planning journey is available at boutiquefitnessbroker.com—a free valuation estimator, educational content on every topic in this book, and information about working with our team. Follow along on Instagram at @boutiquefitnessbrokers for market updates and client success stories, and if you see me at an industry event, come over and say hello.

I offer free consultations—no pitch, no pressure, just a conversation about where you are and what your options might be. Email me at mitch@boutiquefitnessbroker.com or reach out through the website. I respond personally.

WORK WITH QUALIFIED PROFESSIONALS

Find an accountant who has worked on small business sales. Find an attorney who has done dozens of M&A transactions in similar industries at similar prices. Find a broker who has actually sold businesses in your industry. These specialists exist, and they change outcomes.

And if you want to talk to me, I'm here. This is the work I'm supposed to be doing, and every conversation I have makes me better at it. Thank you for reading. Now go make it happen.

— Mitch McGinley, Boutique Fitness Broker
   boutiquefitnessbroker.com
   mitch@boutiquefitnessbroker.com

www.ingramcontent.com/pod-product-compliance
Lightning Source LLC
Chambersburg PA
CBHW062222150726
47991CB00006B/2389